Our Words Our Voices

An Anthology by the writers of Nathaniel Gadsden's Writers Wordshop

ISBN 978-1-893176-34-8

Table of Contents

Introduction

Nathaniel Gadsden's Writers Wordshop a 501(c)(3) organization began as an idea to bring a 'people's poetry venue" to the Harrisburg area. A chance meeting with Mim Warden, founder of the "People Place" Arts Center, lead to the formation of a wonderful relationship with her organization and the birth of Nathaniel Gadsden's Writers Wordshop.

The name Writers Wordshop (which was supposed to be Writers Workshop) was actually a mistake on Mim's part, while she was completing an application to the National Endowment on the Arts. The name "Wordshop" stuck with us and we never let it go. As I was in the process of incorporating the Writers Wordshop, I discovered that there are other organizations name "The Writers Wordshop." On the advice from a good friend, I simply added my name, and our organization was firmly imprinted on the fabric of the Harrisburg area arts scene.

The Writers Wordshop currently has a dynamic Advisory Board and wonderful relationships with Mid-Town Scholar Bookstore, which provides space for our weekly Open Poetry Reading Series, and the Harrisburg Police Athletic League. We also enjoy incredible partnerships with the State Museum of Pennsylvania, which provides us with the use of their venue six times a year to sponsor free programs to the community, and Harrisburg Mall, which teams with us to sponsor a great Pre-Kwanzaa Festival that the whole community embraces.

This Anthology represents the heart of Nathaniel Gadsden's Writers Wordshop. The writings in this collection span over 43 years of personal inspiration, wisdom, insight, and investment of the human spirit. The Poets and Writers in this collection are all "Souls of the Word" who have graced the Writers Wordshop with the blessing of their unique gift – their voice. They are only a small representation of the many who have found the uplifting stage of the Writers Wordshop and used it as a platform to soar with other "Eagles of the Muse." Enjoy this journey of real life, magic, tears, and laughter. The heart of the Wordshop is on display in these pages. Get inspired! Join us on this wonderful voyage! Join Nathaniel Gadsden's Writers Wordshop! Find your voice and share it with the world!

Rev. Dr. Nathaniel J. Gadsden, Founder/Director
pgadsden@aol.com

Dedication

Nathaniel Gadsden, Sr.

Thank you!
The words don't seem to fit the occasion
This occasion
A loving look back
An enthusiastic glance forward
An appreciative smiling face
Words Flashing and rushing forward
Painting pictures
And telling stories
From many cultures and perspectives
From many experiences
And journeys far too fantastic to maintain in a single
imaginative soul
Every word
Every phrase
Every metaphor
Every image
Every Character
Every sound
Every breath
Every day
Every hour
Every minute
Worth every second of my life to be with you
Thank you

I know it's not enough
I say this with humility and respect in my most
poetic voice
I thank you for the years
The tears
The cheers
The formation of our extended family
Orphans and Stepchildren of the Muse
Gathered in a loose-fitting network of mutual,
common, and uncommon, sharing
We mixed colors
And bent lines of gender differences
We crossed the divide of time
Age was a stage but not a barrier
We were odd but brilliantly so
All these years
I have to catch my wind just thinking about all these
years
Faces too many to remember
Stories too many to recite
Words too many to hang onto
And all I have is Thank You
I keep reaching for more
I want to say something worthy of a gathering like
this
I am in an amazing space
1977 to now
The in-between is my dash of poetic splendor-YOU
The reason the Wordshop was given birth
You – The Soul Train Line of Poetry

You – The word writer of the cloud
You – The Joyful noise on a Friday night, in a small room, made translucent by your free-flowing, unselfish genius
You – I thank you
For you have enriched my life, far beyond the reach of my imagination
And I am blessed because of you
The gift that God gave to me
Amen!

While listening to 'HELLO' by Neil Diamond

Ronnie Banks

The most loving word is "hello"
A greeting or beginning
The heart yearns to reveal a secret
free it.
You will be rewarded
From within or by response
Strengthen your soul, heart, and faith

MUSEUM

Ronnie Banks

The walls are dressed
with smiles, favor
and stories of loves and lives
that may guide me, lift me and ultimately
encourage me to forge a path
that is worthy of the children
offer a stone to make it better

AMERICA IS.......

Ronnie Banks

America is not a patch of mud
to be set upon by shelters
not a garden to be cultivated
to feed its masters or its slaves
not a pasture for beasts to roam
and consume its bountiful blessings
it is not the tomb of precious stone and ore
that makes just mans greed
nor is it the guarded domain, where entry
is granted pursuant to the content of one's purse
America is the ideal that will remain
when the mud dries
and the wind carries the dust
to another home
where man will once again "FOLLOW"

FRIEND

Ronnie Banks

It doesn't take a lifetime
To make a friend
A word of kindness
or deed of conscience
can forge a bond
that distance or eternity
cannot disjoin.
To leave and yet remain
Is the miracle of friendship.

Heavenly vigil
Ronnie Banks

We may never look upon the same evening star
Or share the same light of day
But on occasion, I will tilt back my head
And smile toward heaven
That you may see it

Ronnie's favorite activities are writing poetry, singing, and acting. He has been an attendee to NATE GADSDEN WORDSHOP for 20 years, He began acting about the same time for DOROTHY KINGS PENOWL PRODUCTIONS. He has performed in stage productions for Theater Harrisburg, Open Stage Harrisburg, Ollie Milligan Productions staged at Whitaker Center, Freedom Chapel Dinner theater, Christiana Pa, and The Walters Family Dinner Theater, Woodstock, Ontario, Canada.

Our Blackness

Terri Durden

Black Voices Matter...
When we speak our minds
Share our thoughts
Verbalize our truths.

Black Thoughts Matter...
When we think with pride
Dig deep inside
Express how we really feel
Deep down inside.

Black Lives...
Black Men, Black Women,
Black Children, Black Families Matter
When we stand against our oppressors
When we stick together
When we stand our ground
When we have the courage
To speak our truths
Speak our minds
Band together
For the good of
All Black Lives.

Black Art Matters...
If we express our struggles
With paint and pen

On paper and on walls.

Black Art Matters...
When we share our stories
Show the glory
Of All Black men.

Black Voices...
Black Thoughts
Black Lives
Black Art
It All Matters to us,
It's very Relevant to us,
It's a must
To Push Forward our Dreams.

Black Voices Matter...
Black Thoughts Matter
Black Lives Matter
Black Art Matters
To All Black, People, Everywhere!

It helps us...
To Band Together
Be Strong Together...and
Unite as One...because
We're All That Matters
To Us.

There is Value in the Ghetto
Terri Durden

The soul of the Ghetto is deep...
Like roots planted in concrete,
Then blooms into a rose
Through all the stench,
The filth and crime...and
The Ghetto's Soul Lives On.

Did you know,
There is Beauty in the Ghetto?
There is Value in the Ghetto.

The Suburbs ain't got nothin' on the Ghetto,
They ain't got no love...for the Ghetto.

The Ghetto is Vibrant,
It's Lively,
It's full of Color and Song.

There's no time to be wasting,
We've got us some livin' to do!

No pretense,
We keeps it Real!

Cause...Ghetto Lives Matter Too!

There is Beauty in the Ghetto...

These Street-Sounds
Are Our Battleground,
It's Holy ground...and
The Struggle is Real in the Ghetto.

But there is Freedom...
In the day to day Struggle,
It's our Learning Tree.

There is Beauty in the Ghetto...
There is Value in the Ghetto,
It's where Laughter
Reverberates off the walls...and
Crushes Hate.

The Mixing & Mingling
Of Third-World Collaborators.

It's where healing takes place
Amongst the Rat-Race.

Them Streets Ain't Loyal,
But that Ghetto-Love
Can't be beat!

There is Beauty in the Ghetto...
There is Value in the Ghetto,
Lessons are Learned in the Ghetto,
Knowledge is Attained in the Ghetto.

While Aiming at your Jugular,
This Predator,
Opens Third-Eye Doors
For those who Crave More.

The Ghetto is filled with
Social-Loco Creatives...and
The Vibe,
It's all the way Live!

It's filled with...
BeUtiful Brown Faces,
Black Faces,
Red and Yellow Faces Too.

Come Witness its Splendor and Glory...
Intermingled with Angst.

Identities and False Realities
Of Experimented Lives...

Injecting Music in Our Veins
The Love of the Ghetto
Sears Our Brains...and
Our Souls are On Fya!

There is Beauty in the Ghetto...
There is Value in the Ghetto,
It passes down something so Spiritual
So Volatile and Soothing.

There's something so Real
About the Ghetto,
That makes you Feel,
Makes you Heal,
Livin' in the Ghetto
It's Surreal.

There is Beauty in the Ghetto...
There is Value in the Ghetto,
You become Awakened in the Ghetto,
There's no Escaping the Lessons taught,
The Knowledge Gaines,
The Struggle,
The Strain...and
Many Years of Pain in the Ghetto.

The Ghetto has Purpose...
It has Feelings,
Past and Present.

The Ghetto is Filled with...
Loud-Talk and Hip-Hop,
Murder, Death, Rhythm and Blue.

It's Filled with...
Jazz, Funk, Dope fiends and Drunks.

It's Filled with...
Our Peeps,

But it's got a Love so Deep,
With Children up & down the Streets,
The Soul of the Ghetto is Deep.

There's a Rhythm to these Streets,
Catch the Beat...and Soar!

Love & Regret Live in the Ghetto...and
Yet, the Ghetto you won 'the soon forget.

It's a Life Experienced Experiment.

Preserving and Extracting,
Distracting and Detracting,
Exacting Wrongs.

There is Beauty in the Ghetto...
The Ghetto has Value.

It's Art & Activism,
Politics & Grit,
Filth & Shit.

It's Lust & Forbidden Fruit,
It's Jazz & Blues,
It's Gangsta-Rap strollin' down the Avenue.

There is Beauty in the Ghetto...
There is Value in the Ghetto,
The Ghetto...made me who I Am.

It's Hip-Hop & Slick,
Legit & Counterfeit,
El Barrio & Chinatown,
It's the Get-Down, Funky-Town,
With Bullets Flyin' Round.

It's Sweat Shops & Locs,
Fried Fish & Cornbread.

It's Craps & Crack, Posted up beside
Watermelon market stands...and
A Corner Bodega.

It's Bean Pies...and The Call,
With a Church and Bar on every other Corner.

There is Beauty in the Ghetto...
There is Value in the Ghetto,
The Street Cries,
Then Orchestrates Lullaby's.

In the Ghetto...
Dreams ain't supposed to Die a Natural Death.

In order to See it,
You must Live it,
Then Believe in it.

You've got to be there...

In the Early Morning Light...or
Late into the Wee Hours of the Night.

Surviving Life...
Is a Lesson Taught in the Ghetto,
We Thrive in the Ghetto.

And... if you Don't Know, Now you Know!

There is Beauty in the Ghetto...
There is Value in the Ghetto,
It's a Hard-Life, Well-Lived,
That we're too Joyous
To be Boxex-In.

So... Come on in...
Take a Peek,
Feel the Vibe...of the Ghetto Streets.

This Kitchen

Terri Durden

This Kitchen...
It was a sacred place
For Families
To Learn, to Grow,
To Teach and Preach from,
To Pray...and
Shoulder-Lean,
To Live, Laugh and Love in.

This Kitchen...
Holds many secrets
It's where various stories were told.

This Kitchen...
Hearts and minds were filled,
Some soul exchanging took place.

This Kitchen...
Was Grandma's Domain,
It's where she created a succulent feast!
With wonderful smell wafting through the air.

Some scrubbing of floors,
Washing and drying dishes...and
Wiping away tears.

This Kitchen...

Is where Grandma Reigned Supreme,
Teaching the Rules to Live by,
Sharing Recipes,
To Stand Tall and Grow by,
Molding Beautiful Minds,
Imparting Wisdom.

This Kitchen...
It's where we were Schooled,
Taught the Golden Rules...and
Socialized in it.

We handled business in it!
Held our Family Together in it,
Gained Friends in it,
It was the Heartbeat of Our Home.

This Kitchen...
Is where we Gravitate,
Filled Our Plates,
With much more than Food,
There was Knowledge to be Gained,
Traditions to be Passed Down.

In This Kitchen...
Masterpieces were Created,
Self-Esteem was Built,
Great Leaders were Born,
Important Conversations...and
Some Really Good Gossip was heard,

Church Hymns were Sung,
Real-Talk...and
Some Tell it Like it Is
Was a Must!

If These Walls Could Talk...
Oh! The many Stories they would Tell.

In This Kitchen...
We not only handled Family Business,
We discussed Community Business...and
Current Affairs,
Watched and discussed the News...and
Black History in it.

In This Kitchen...
From the Window
She would Oversee
The Children in the Neighborhood.

In This Kitchen...
We handled our Grief,
As well as the Grief of Others,
Spoke Our Truths in it.

In This Kitchen...
We Taught as well as
We made History in it.

We Blazed Trails...

Mended Hearts and Souls,
Chartered Courses,
Passed Down Life Lessons,
It's where Miracles were Born.

In This Kitchen...
This Sacred Place,
Filled with Many Memories...and
Love.

It's a Place where Dreams were Conceived,
It's where Families Grow from,
Homework was done in it.

It's where Grandma
Preached & Prayed.

It's where Our Lives Begin,
We Lived, Laughed, Loved...and
Shoulder-Leaned in it.

God Bless This Kitchen.

Dedicated To: Ms. Beattie for David Cruz Jr.

Waiting to be Born

Terri Durden

A little Black Girl
Is waiting to be born.

I can see the Congo in her eyes.
Egypt in her soul...
With the heart of a Lion.

There is Africa all up in this!

From Nigeria to Sierra Leone
From her Rowandian strut
To that Ghana dip in her hips.

There is Africa all up in this!

All of this magnificence...She is,
Royalty crowned gracefully.

There is Africa all up in this!

Somewhere out there...
A little Black Girl
She is waiting
To be Born.

From the Beauty in her Zimbabwe face,
To the curves of her Somalian waist,

The warmth of the shimmer
In her Golden-Brown Sudanese skin.

There is Egypt in her soul.

From Mali to Uganda
From Liberia to Senegal
Such Beauty
Such grace.

A little Black Girl
She is waiting...somewhere
In Kenya to be Born
Black, Beautiful and Free!

I see Africa in her Soul...
While walking the Streets of Harlem.

While Cooking in Restaurant Kitchens
While Teaching School...and
Tending to someone else's Children.

While waiting in Welfare Lines...or
Serving in Soup Kitchens.

While Baking Bread or
Braiding Hair.

I can see...
Behind her eyes

The Heartland
The Motherland
Glistens in her soul
Shines Bright
Like Sun in your eyes.

From the Gleam of her Teeth
The Strength in her Thighs
The Arch of her Back
The Love in her Smile
The Want of her Care
The Coil of her Hair.

There is Africa all up in this!

I can see it in Her Soul...and
Somewhere, out there
A little Black Girl
She is Waiting
To be Born.

Terri Durden is a Consciousness Poet/Collage Artist…who Blends Art and words… She uses the voice of an African American Woman to speak to all people about issues of Universal importance that are most often ignored by our TV/Drama society. She has written several Plays including a production that was performed at the world famous "Fulton Opera House". The play entitled "Our People Are Going Up In Smoke" a play on the overwhelming epidemic of Crack-Cocaine that has plagued our nation. Toured Pennsylvania youth and correctional and drug rehabilitation institutions. Terri has performed in many as well as she has written/ directed/choreographed plays and dance/poetry numbers/Taught youth Collage Art & Photography Card making for community organizations, Churches, Schools, Colleges and Universities…such as Franklin and Marshall College, Millersville University, Penns-Landing Philadelphia, PA. The Serengeti Café' and Jazz Club New Jersey…with many performances in New York, New Jersey, Northern California. Lancaster, West Chester, York, Harrisburg, Reading and Philadelphia Pennsylvania. Current Judge for "Lancaster Youth Poet Laureate" through a partnership between "Lancaster Community Foundation" and "The Mix at Arbor Place". Terri is the Author of 3 books of poetry with a new collection Released in 2016 entitled: "Word-Sounds Echoing" The Poetic Ramblings, and Photography of: Terri A. Durden. Terri has been working on a Fact-based Fiction about Michael Jackson as well.

A Lion's Pride

Lunden McClain

What is it to be a man?
To be strong and fearless?
What is Mufasa masculinity,
When not fishbone fragile?
What is it to be framed head of a household,
Like the head of a table or the head above a mantle?
To be the only bull in a herd of heifers?
Who knows what it is like?
To be surrounded by the weak.

What is it to be a man?
Who was taught to never cry?
And therefore he does not know
What tears look like
When he causes them to fall?
From Jane Doe deer eyes.

What is it to be a man?
Who was taught that he?
Was as brave as a lion?
How his roar shook Sharabi's trees,
Made her body crumble like
The blood red leaves of autumn.
How his long flowing mane,
Made him invincible.
And how he was taught that

He was the king of the jungle,

As all the pretty gazelles and giraffes
Grazed green grasslands.
They are just a pair of long legs to devour.
They, a contoured torso,
A corpse to consume.
And when he has learned that he can hunt
His prey whenever he pleases,
Has learned to leave the bones of butchered women
Stuck inside the slits of his teeth.
And use his claws as a toothpick.
As he is congratulated for every kill,
For everybody he has caught,
You cannot blame him for winning.
Because it's only primal instinct,
Only natural.
This is what he has been groomed to do
Since he was a cub:
Hunt.

But sadly, lions are becoming
Endangered all of a sudden.
How they've become more sniper than snarl,
More silent than snicker.
And what is a lion that now has more scars
Then the survivors who escaped his grasp?

3rd Time's a Charm
Lunden McClain

We were 3/5ths.
Always compromising for someone else's benefit.
Never got to speak.
Never got a say.
Or a seat at the table,
But now we're 13.
13% of the population.
50% of the crime rate.
Half of the issues that affect us are not our fault.
There's a lot of division in our systems.
And there's a lot of division in the system,
But how the pie was never divided in our favor.
How some kids weren't even taught pie square.
How most kids hate math, when we invented it.
Hate math 'cause it will "never be relevant"
But if 400 years
Divided by
46 million slaves
Equals
Over 42 million blacks with deep rooted trauma,
Then why are we the ones that are forced to face
inequality?
More like everyday reality.
That is, what used to be our everyday reality for
centuries,

Which seems to be so long ago that everyone
doesn't remember.
Or do they choose to forget?
Are we the forgotten ones?
Hanging onto this country's flag pole
By a nylon colored noose that's been decorated like a
string.
Or maybe we are the scribes,
A black dot planted on a bed of white lies
Or are we really the stripes?
Yet these look more like prison bars from the inside,
'Cause our lives are always on the line.
Have to always walk the line like a sobriety test
tightrope.
Always being pulled over.
And pushed down.
And pulled underwater, knowing we can't swim.
Still trying to sink us knowing we'll resurface,
And they still try to sting us?
Like your hands after a tug of war.
This is a tug of war.
This is an internal war.
This is an eternal war
That might make the public go crazy inward,
Like we were in a ward-
But when will it end?
Because if 3rd time's the charm,
And 3rd place is always last,
Then what are we?

Strongest Thing You Can Do

Lunden McClain

To be a brown girl means to
Be the strongest person in the room.
To be a girl means to
Always have to smile
Even when you don't want to.
To always have to laugh
Even when you don't think things are funny.
Always have to stand your ground,
Even when they say you're wrong.

To be a girl means
You have to be competitive with so many other girls.
To pin one person against another,
To hate someone, knowing nothing about her-
But you have to be the one that
Gets through that doorway.
That "gets the job",
That "gets the guy",
To even get on their level,
You must knock everyone else down who crosses your
path.
If someone else wins,
We never take a chance to celebrate it.

To be a brown girl
You must be able to take a compliment.

To say thank you, to be grateful.
Have to always make them feel
As if they are doing you a favor
By reminding you what you already know.

To be a brown girl is to be walked over.
To always have to work harder than everyone else
And yet never get the credit-
And still you must be content with that.

To be a girl means
You have to be able to want to create life
Within your own body.
To be ready to be a mother,
To take care of another human being,
When you can barely take care of yourself,
And if you're not ready
You will be shamed for that too.

You have to be ready for whatever punches
The world may throw your way
Without skipping a beat,
Because that's what is expected of you.
To be put together and never fall apart.
To be powerful and yet
Fragile all at the same time.

BUT
To be a brown girl is in fact
The strongest thing you can do

Because no one knows
What it is like to be that girl.
No one understands
The struggle of everyday looking in the mirror
And feeling not good enough.
They don't know the pressure to be perfect
As you look at your cell phone screen
As you are consistently told you aren't beautiful.
To be told you are never enough.

What it's like to wake up every day
Having to face criticism,
Racism,
Colorism,
As soon as you look online.
As soon as you step out the door.
As soon as you go to school.
And soon as you come right back home.
It's so hard to be everything all at once,
It gets so hard to keep up with who society
Believes you should and shouldn't be.

But when you know they are wrong about you,
You are greater.
You are who you are now
And what you dream to be.
You are more than just a body,
Or a pretty face,
Or the way you dress.
More than the color of your skin

And nothing can stop you or
Take you away from your destiny.
Whatever obstacle that is in your way
It is just something to prepare you for the next one.
It is just something that is making you stronger.
It is just something to show you
That you are capable of anything
That you can imagine.

So go on.
Prove them wrong.
Take a stand in your own truth.
Take a stand in your own skin.
Be who you want and what you want to be
Without the hesitation of someone else's thinking.

Be a model.
Be a firefighter.
Be a beautician.
Be a designer.
Be a technician and a plumber.
Be an architect and an astronaut.
Be a police officer and a scientist.
Or a doctor and an engineer.
Be a lawyer and an author.
Be a singer and a dancer.
Be a zoologist and veterinarian.
Be a mother or not a mother at all.
Be a dreamer and be braver.
And be happy and know that it's ok to not always be.

Speak loudly.
And don't settle.
And take up space.
And say no.
And don't apologize for saying no.

Let your hair grow.
Cut it off.
And let it grow again.
And wear a skirt.
And wear a suit.
And be a slob.
And be a boss.
And be the queen
And the king of the castle.
Be confident.
And be selfish.
And love yourself.
And be anything,
Or anyone you feel like being.
Be all of these things.

Be a brown girl.
And be a brown woman.
And know that it's okay
To be that girl first
Before you become that woman.
Take your time in finding
The person you want to be.
And do it for yourself.

And be the strongest person in the room,
Without having to trample over any of your sisters.

I'm looking at you now.
I can see you're already doing it.
You're already braver.
You're already beautiful.
Already kind.
And smart.
And enough.
You are already enough.
You are already enough.
You are already enough.
Hey girl,
YES.
YOU.
YOU are already enough.

Because you are already you.
So when you don't have to change being you,
For anyone-
I think,
That's the strongest thing you can do.

Playground Rulez

Lunden McClain

I went for a walk
To my old elementary school park
The other day.
My inner child leaping out of my body
As I darted for the best-looking banana boat swing
Before anyone else could snag it,

Grabbing one hell of a tetanus shot in one palm
And a layer of kindergarten snot in the other,
I gave myself a swinging start.
Clasping onto rusting chains,
Ones that had stood the test of time
For a thousand years,
Through rainstorms, and 5th grade brawls
That swing set has seen it all.

And when I saw a group of boys
Playing on the wooden jungle gym,
The memories started flooding in
Like chatty students on a Wednesday morning.
I imagined bubbles, and rainbows,
And snacks galore
I mean,
This playground was where whimsy was born!
Where imagination literally ran wild,
On seesaws
In empty grass fields,

And dirt patches made for kickball.

The boys,
Laughing and playing
Sticks in hand, it seems like
They are ready for a pirate's sword fight,
Firemen poles turn into vines,
Monkey bars turn into tests of strength,
Metal equipment turned into a gymnast's paradise,
A tree into a mountain,
Sidewalk chalk into DaVinci's paint brush,
My legs into mom's spaghetti
As I go higher, and higher, and hi-

Suddenly, the sound of gun clips emptying
Makes my skin jump off the swing.
Bullets fly into the air like
Black crows on a Sunday afternoon.
My little-girl-self gets down,
As if it were an inside intruder drill.
And there was an intruder,
This fear inside my body constantly striking me in
the heart-
But no child in sight moves a muscle.
Not one boy flinches or falls to the ground.

I turn my body around
To see more bullets ricocheting
Off of metal pillars,
Pillars that hold up wooden bridges,

Bridges that hold up paper children.
The same boys who I thought would grow up to be pirates
Have found a better game to play-
And for a moment,
I question why I am so scared of
Branches shaped like AK7s.
Of little boys holding sticks
As if they were army rifles.

How their big bangs and lip trills
Make it all sound like it's all real.
Another clip empties,
One boy decides to count to ten
As he reloads with his eyes closed.
The other boys ready their weapons-
Two of them stand watch on the bridge.
They aren't scared like I am,
They aren't scared to die or hide.
The last one takes cover under an aluminum slide,
They laugh and giggle
With their guns in their hands.
Three boys run down from the jungle gym
And swiss army knife their way to cover-
Elbows in soil, and mud-covered cheekbones.

And I have never witnessed something so jarring-
Never seen anything so alarming,
Because I know it isn't real.
They are just sticks, and sound effects,

Mulch disguised as bombed sand dunes,
Tree bark as smoke screens,
But I can't help but really think
Like, "is this what we are teaching our youth?"
To see the news, as another battlefield,
Real life events as a game of battleship,
Or Call of Duty?
Is it not our **call** and duty to tell them when
A game has gone too far.
Why students are dying in stores, on floors,
At school, at festivals, in theatres or in bars?

For now,
Their sticks are shaped like guns,
But in a few years
Will their guns just look like sticks?
Like harmless, normal things
That stem from violent trees-
Regenerated health after every death
And still act like these hearts don't break?
If we don't speak up, then no one will.
Will we act like it's not as bad it seems
Be all, a made-up game
Like pirates on a ship at sea,
Like gun violence is all just a prank-
And if so, will your life, too
Have to walk the plank?

Dog Days of Summer

Lunden McClain

It's the same every time-
Just a different boy,
Another bowl food body
Hanging from some tree,
Dumped in some river,
Laying dead on some unknown street
In a puddle of its own blood,
Another black soul stripped
Of all the life within it
But still, the world keeps spinning.

Keeps rising
Like a sun,
Like a son...
Too small to reach the cotton gin fan
Boy Scout bound around his neck.
Too small to stop the heavy bullet
Borrowing its way inside his head.
Too black to stop the blood from streaming
Down his star boy skin.
How he can have his summer,
How he can be a star,
As long as he is a burning dead thing
In the sultry stratosphere
Far away from anyone else's rocket man reach.

And isn't that so funny?
How we will always be the "dawg" that whistles,
The mutt that barks
On a leash made of chains-
One that suffocates its own throat
Whenever it moves its shackled paws.
The body belonging in a barbed wire cage.
Back hunched, breaking its mold to fit-
I mean sit, nice and Mastiff muzzle silent.

How something so brown,
Can be so clean,
And yet was put down
For just breathing.
For just walking down the street
Without its chains,
Without its leash,
Without its owner to tug,
To yank,
To remind him
That he will always be an animal,
That he will always be a pet-
Something to control
With trap doors and treats,
With trick laws and legislation
That make his breed feel safe
When they are being hunted every day.

And isn't that so funny,
How he was euthanized?

How in his youth, they gouged out his eyes
And put him to death so "humanly"?
By boiling his bloated body,
Cooking his scalp into a brainstem stew
The bowl his battered skull.
Why do they keep coming back for seconds?
Why do they keep coming back for seconds?
Why do they keep coming back for seconds?
Killing now, for the sport of it and
How at some point, it was all just practice,
But how all boyish blood has to spill
That Emmett Till color
Doesn't it?

But it's funny
How a mother can wail like that.
How her voice can crack so hard
And so raw like rock fragmented.
Her windpipe bursts open like a fresh body does,
As she sits there,
Pacing, crying, howling at the moon
For her child to come crawling home,
To run home,
To stay home,
Stay here where he is alive,
Again and again and again each time,
But then, he doesn't.

And it's the same every time—
Just a different boy,

Another bowl food body
Locked away in some cage,
Laying down dead in some forest,
Shot in some unknown city
In a puddle of its own blood-
Whelp, just a pup,
Belly up, and whimpering.
Just another black soul stripped
Of all the life within it.

And still, the world keeps spinning.
The sun keeps rising,
But how we have too many
Dying sons in our entire dire solar system.
Huh,
I thought you would have found that one funny.
Why aren't you laughing yet?

Bio: Lunden McClain has always been a creative
spirit. From dancing and acting to singing and
playing instruments, she has been expressing
herself through art, so there was no surprise when
she started writing and performing poetry last
Spring. Even though she hasn't been writing for
long, she uses her talents to write about important
topics in society.

The Environmental Phobias

Daniel Snowden

Ah, the need to preserve the environment
The lengths that some people will go
To prevent any type of development
From encroaching upon nature's show.

However, there are many persons out there
Who would pull out all the stops
They are the Environmental Phobias
For the record, all are tops.

First, there are the NIMBYs
Or the Not-in-my-Back Yard types
These are the best-known phobias
And the ones that get the most hype.

Next on the list we have the BANANAs
Build Absolutely Nothing Anywhere Near Anybody
This is a flat impossibility
Which could just wind up infuriating most
everybody.

We also have the CAVEs
Citizens Against Virtually Everything
These persons do mean well
But fall far short of accomplishing anything.

Last, there are the LULUs

Locally Unwanted Land Uses
These depict things rather than people
And tend to bring collective refuses.

Environmental Phobias are not all bad
They just need an opposite partner
Once sound cooperation takes place among these
All parties may end up the smarter.

Waste Management Done Right
Daniel Snowden

Humanity creates all types of wastes
That occur in many shapes and sizes
Yet the management of these substances
Takes much effort to earn any prizes.

Waste management is by no means easy
The task requires sound execution
As such, when wastes receive utmost attention
Their stages are set for revolution.

So what steps are taken to manage wastes?
A good starting point is generation
Where wastes are initially created
Throughout each and every single nation.

Since there is a real need to manage wastes
Making less of these works well any day
This simple concept is called REDUCTION
The first waste management stage every way.

Some things are called wastes after a short time
When their useful lives are deemed ended
Yet many items have second chances
For REUSE, as innovates intended.

Some materials have a special trait
Keeping their substances while changing forms

Paper, plastic, glass, metals, organics
Are RECYCLABLE, following their norms.

When all waste management options are spent
Reduce, reuse, and recycle as well
The small amounts of wastes still left over
Are slated for final DISPOSAL, do tell.

Thus the varied steps in waste management
Paint a vivid picture with sharp insight
Waste management, more INTEGRATED now
Qualifies as waste management done right.

Geology and Life
Daniel Snowden

The science of geology
Supports all of life upon planet Earth
Without its consummate presence
Humans, flora, and fauna have no berth.

If there were no geology
Then no materials or energy sources would be
Thus, it pays for all of us
To give this science a much more closer see.

More importantly, without geology
Water resources would be no more
And society as we know it
Would soon follow out of the same door.

Again, if no geology were here
To help with understanding natural disasters
All persons who live on planet Earth
Would meet their collective demise all the faster.

These are but a few examples
Of geology's role in life
Perhaps taking this science more seriously
Could lead to worlds of less strife.

Life's Lemons: No Thank You!

Daniel Snowden

How often has this common phrase been said
"When life hands you lemons, make lemonade"
Okay, but one should also consider
Other "foods" that make or surpass the grade.

Life is often difficult and unfair
In spite of the efforts that are given
To make the best of bad situations
Which come, no matter how well we're driven.

Sometimes we can take life's lemons quite far
Using creative manipulation
Transforming many a disappointment
Into items of great fascination.

However, it is worthwhile to note
Life's lemons are not always meant to "take"
Lemon-based "drinks," "desserts" and other things
Cannot serve as the only "foods" to make.

There are always a few alternatives
To accepting life's lemons as they're cast
Turing them into other things palatable
By bringing in other items – a blast!

Life's lemons really need to be set aside
To allow more outcome diversity

Let's have all other "foods" available
For quelling all manner of travesty.

This person plans to place life's lemons
With "farther along" and "by and by," too
If they really don't need to be present
To life's lemons, I say, No Thank You!

Approaches to Solving Problems
Daniel Snowden

Sooner or later, we'll all have problems
Which may last for the short term, or the long
The methods that are used to resolve these
Should be numerous and, made very strong.

Problems may receive their resolutions
Even before they can ever be born
In this case, planning and perseverance
Can ensure that problems are never worn.

Another way to approach these problems
Is encountering them at their sources
Here, the problem can become starved of food
Which then leads them, from us, to divorces.

Those pesky problems can also be met
By opposing forces, after they've spread
In applying the proper mix of tools
The problems shall likely wind up quite dead.

There are times when problems become so large
That more than one approach may be needed
Thus, using multiple, resolving tricks
Make for problems' whims going unheeded.

As shown here, problems are ubiquitous
Making us all quite exasperated
Yet, once the shared resolutions are used
Problems are just best eviscerated!

Dr. Daniel E. Snowden is a regular attendee of the Writers' Wordshop and this is where he learned how to write poetry. His poems generally cover science and nature topics, but he has written some poems that involve some social commentary. Dr. Snowden resides in Harrisburg, PA and is a long-time employee with the Commonwealth of Pennsylvania (currently with the PA Department of Environmental Protection). Dr. Snowden has a B. A. in Geology from La Salle University (1987) and, both an M. S. in Mineral Economics (1989) and a D.Ed. in Curriculum and Instruction (Science Education/Earth and Environmental Sciences) (2009) from the Pennsylvania State University.

Queen

Jasmira Hunter

We have become tired,
Trying to love and protect our brethren
We have become worn
Yes, we took a little for ourselves
But it wasn't enough
In doing for the world
We forgot about our stuff, our wants and yes, our
needs
Without trying
We became women who please.
Make do women.
Who figure it out
Make do women
With little to no clout
We hustled
We made a dollar
Out of 15 cents
We cried
We screamed
And we still paid the rent
For a long time we went without
Holding our breath
Not quite sure when to let it out
We extinguished fires
That we should have let burn
We loved in spite of being spurned

We held ourselves
Even made ourselves
Come
When we should had someone else get it done.
We did too much for those we loved and who we
thought loved us
But we have been told it's in God we put our trust
So now we're finding and accepting peace
No longer bowing down
We're finally putting back on our crowns

So You're Getting Married?
Jasmira Hunter

So You're getting Married?
How exciting for you?
I hate to be the bearer of bad news. Lend me your
ear for a moment, and your brain and your heart,
because this is life changing, you have to be smart.
You think you're in love, so, what I'm about to say
will sound like hate.
But deep in your heart, you know you should wait.
You're getting married, even bought yourself a ring,
the man who loves you would do that sort of thing.
Didn't he just get out of jail after doing a 5-year
bid?
You're going to go through hell if you go through
with this kid.
I know he says he loves you and hearing it makes you
smile
but how does his actions make you feel?
Go ahead, think on it awhile.
You already know the answer, or you wouldn't be
about to cry.
You're right he's not in love with you
let me tell you why.
You never tell him no
You answer his every call
You're there at a moment's notice
He doesn't miss you at all

You do everything for yourself
Proving you don't need him
Yeah, he knows you love him, he has no doubts about that
Because you've moved heaven and earth for him, he doesn't know how to love you back.
He's shown you he's not capable of being who you need.
He's even given you tests, hoping you'll succeed
but you fail them every time proving you're a fool
So eventually it'll become easy, your strings for him to pull
He'll begin to use you.
Even at times laugh at your love.
It'll become a joke to him.
You're putting him above yourself and everyone; even your career.
It'll end when he's had enough of not loving you, my dear.
I know you saw the movies

And Listened to the songs
Figured you'd get the fairytale if you just played along
I know every situation is different but if anything I said rings true, he's not worth what you are allowing him to put you through.
Do yourself a favor and be strong enough to end it now, or you'll spend a whole lot of time recovering from being his clown.

Always Yours

Jasmira Hunter

We were always yours
 It does not matter what he said, what he did, what
he didn't do
We were always yours: to love, hold, nurture and
raise
Who he was with; how it affected you should not
have changed your love for us.
We were always yours: to love protect respect and
care for.
It does not matter what happened with him.
You were given 2 precious gifts
Your childhood, your life, your hurt, your pain; God
can heal you
Your life, your goals, your efforts, your sacrifices,
don't let that be in vain.
We are still yours God's most precious gifts.
It's not too late

The Conscious Mind

Jasmira Hunter

Trust me with your poison don't push me away with
your fear!
Looking in a mirror, are any of us happy here?
We make it through the hour we make it through
the day
We can't seem to make it through or get out of our
own way.
We cry when someone dies
We cry when babies are born
We laugh if we find something humorous
But through it all we are torn
Are we really happy?
Do we know what it means?
Does our happiness only live in our dreams?
We say goodbye to loved ones as they age and pass
away
While conscious of the fact that soon will be our day
We walk through this life
Sometimes with a blank stare
All the while wondering who really cares?

Men Have Been Hurt Too

Jasmira Hunter

Toxic, hurt, insecure women are raising boys, who
are now men
doing their best to ignore
the noise women make, scream, and say
claiming they are the only one who feels this way.
men open up and share some.
you get in a fight and here it comes.
You spew his words
he thought, he could say
to win the fight, to get your way
your family knows all he shared,
he told you because he felt you cared
you tell him he doesn't talk or open up
when he does you use it to kick his butt
listen chick deal with your pain your hurt,
insecurities
or runaround asking yourself
why'd he leave me?

Dummy!

You want him to call you Queen
but when you're angry
you're oh so mean
then another woman gets in between
and treats him like a king

you tell others he's a bum
his new life is upsetting
Because you weren't the one
you don't shout that you're a queen
you're now learning what it means
to have loved and lost
but it wasn't love at all
love doesn't bite nor does it sting
it's honest above all things
do the work or remain insecure
repeating patterns
closing doors
blaming others
when the faults your own
mentally a child
physically full grown

Jasmira L. Hunter, Commonwealth of PA employee of 20 years responsible for assisting with needs in the Bureau of Forestry's Forest Health Division to protect Pennsylvania's forest against invasive species. Project management and some grant writing work. Currently writing 2 books; one of poetry the other of short stories. Jasmira is currently a student at the University of Phoenix working towards her bachelor's degree in business. In her free time she enjoys crocheting. To see some of her work and to place an order please visit her Instagram: @makeaslipknot. Also visit her blog: https://miraticiasthoughts.blogspot.com

This is not a Poem about the Rain

James Roethlein

This is not a poem about the rain
insomuch as to what the rain is doing,
but rather a poem about what it is not,
and what is not,
is coming down handsomely; somewhere else.
It is also not coming down on a day other than
Monday,
which as it happens is today,
so, I know I'll be twice as depressed
My two cats, who care nothing
for what the rain is not doing,
are regarding me as they always do:
as their scratching post, chew toy,
the bringer of their food.
and due to the liquid nature of the weather,
I'm cooped up with them on my day off,
waiting for the rain to do,
what it is not.

After a Storm, Spring 1987
James Roethlein

Rainclouds retreating in the distance,
leaving the world outside my window,
peaceful in its wake.
And I wonder,
is this what it was like in London,
when the dust settled
after the final German rocket fell

Mansion of Memories
James Roethlein

These four walls,
no longer mine.
The mansion of my memories
is letting me go,
that it may adopt a new family.
As the chapter wanes,
the page turns to a new season,
and a new home
that will call me its own.

Phather Phantasm

James Roethlein

Half-seen in my half-stare,
half-believing you are there.
Faded memories and faded thoughts,
raindrops falling on sun-seared rock,
quickly come, and quickly part.
I was eleven when you did not die.
you took your leave, never saying goodbye.
And I, the fool, follow the fool
walking barefoot on broken glass,
and tread upon the blood-stained shards,
waiting to wound me ere I pass.

Kingdom of Crayons

James Roethlein

In the kingdom of crayons
it's midnight blue against black,
and we all follow suit,
going to war
with different hues of wax.
An orange face
an orange face,
to place our blames upon.
All the while the Devil's
on the inside looking in,
and he is laughing
laughing
laughing.

Jim has been writing for almost 25 years and has
been published in Australia, Canada, and the
United States. He is the author of two books
Musing on the Cricket Game of Life, Part 1 1/2
and An Extravagant Way of Saying Nothing. Jim
currently resides in Middletown with his two
cats.

Then and Now

Nathaniel Gadsden

We must choose our battles wisely to ensure
success both individually and collectively.
Success...I thought about it all day long!
24 hours
1,440 minutes
86,400 seconds of my life.
Trying to control my thoughts
Everyday learning what things are healthy for my
mind, body, and spirit, and putting all my focus on
them constantly...searching for success, like
rock=solid, un-moveable, no doubt about it success.
One full day
Every minute
Every second
Every hour
Of one full day of my life
I thought about, but I couldn't define it.
My vision, dreams, imaginations were full of past and
present steps, missed steps, and relationships that
equal ill-tempered, wanton emotional failure.
Success...I can't form a picture of it in my mind
I'm drifting, log jammed with negative thoughts,
wasting my time
One full day – wasted
The voice of God sounding like Maya Angelou

Speaks to me – shaking the ground beneath me and
swirling the clouds above me God says, Afrikans
reinforce positive thought with appropriate behavior
and cast out all negative conditionings
Why do you bleed your blessing on useless
appendages, like worry and self-doubt.
Give your time to me – Let go
Gain knowledge of yourself
Learn your truth and follow it.
Stay on the path your ancestors blazed for you
Follow the lighted trail of blood, tears, and
determination
Commit to the struggle that surrounds you
Let go of the self-made struggle from within
You are already successful
Speak to your ancestors – they are listening and
watching always
They will tell you the truth that is yours
Let go of the "I" and grab-hold to the "We" as if you
are holding Gold.
Discover who you really are
You didn't know it then – wasting your time
But know it now.
You can't get back then, don't waste your time
trying.
It was then that you made hollow, empty excuses
It was then that you looked for dead, washed-up
scapegoats to devour

It was then that you stopped growing like a jagged-edged stump deep in the forest of lifelessness –
alone
God said, like a broken alarm clock your time stood still
Wake-up
My time for you is moving faster than you can run
You are holding a baton in your hand – don't drop it
You are a magnificent leg in a vast relay race
You are a force of nature – a part of a gargantuan spiritual body that is guided by my light – stay the course.
Forget about then – the wasted time searching for success
Become one with your Now – know that I am with you always
Your ancestors are with me
Stay in your lane – success is in your DNA
Grip the baton of life
Stay woke, lean forward, be ready to pass it on –
your success is in your hand –
Now!!

I See You
Nathaniel Gadsden

I see you!
Fist in my face!
Long thin razor slicing my throat!
My lifeless, mutilated body chained and drugged
behind your old rusty pick-up truck, which is covered
in backwoods dust and poverty stains!

I see you sniffing the air as if a dog just crapped on
your well-worn shoes!
You sniff and frown and stare at me, like I am a
decaying, rotten, stinky corpse invading your holy
space!
You mumble through cracked, barely parted lips, low
enough not to be heard, but felt enough to hurt the
spirit of any one paying attention.
You smell like fresh scaled fish, and month old
chicken livers, left in a hot August sun but you sniff
the air surrounding us, searching me with dead,
soulless eyes, as if to say, Nigga, you make me sick!!

I see you!!
You are trapped in a dream deferred, a dream
denied, a nightmare called Amerikkka.
You were told and sold a Bill of Rights and given a
substitution for the Constitution that informed you
that you were and are better than me.

Better Educated!
Better civilized!
Better culture!
Harder working!
Better skills!
Better relationship with God!
Better regards for life and all that is sacred!
From birth to this very moment of our encounter,
you were told that you are better than me, blessed
and highly favored!
Now that the truth of the lie that you have lived all
these years is uncovered, naked and exposed for all
to see, even you, you are constantly searching for a
reason to dismiss and diminish me.
In order to make this right, you convince yourself
that I must have cheated, the order of nature,
God's divine plan for mankind!

I see you, both inside and out!
No need to envy me. If you really knew how difficult
it is to wear my shoes, you no doubt would not want
to walk in them.
No need to long for the fine clothes I wear, each
thread I earned at great cost. The price almost
killed me!
No need trying to show me how much you hate me,
because I see you wishing you were me, and hating
yourself because the feeling won't go away. So you
stay, stuck in the fantasy of Better-Better land! In

your fantasy, you are better than me no matter what the reality!

I see you!
So I just smile and walk away, and I am all the Better for it!!
But be warned, tomorrow may be different, I'm just saying!

PAIN / PAIN

Rev. Dr. Nathaniel Gadsden

I can't breathe!
I can't breathe!
Ma Ma!!
Ma Ma!!
What's my name?
Eric Garner, Yvette Smith, Alton Sterling, Pamela
Turner, Freddie Gray Jr.,
White silence is violence!
Black lives matter! BLM let's say it again – Black lives
matter!!
I'm going to twist off my foot / turn it in a clockwise
direction until it snaps!
I think I'll twist off my right foot / that's the one I
like best.
I'll turn it slowly in a clockwise direction causing the
veins to pop and the cartilage to snap!
I want the bone to push through the skin / exposing
the white side of my black
self.
I want the blood to gush and the foot to turn a dark
purple.
I want it to make a clean break / and hang gently by
a thin strip of skin!
What's my name?
George Floyd, Janet Wilson, Michael Brown Jr., Mya
Hall, Tamir Rice

I hope "A Jury of my Peers" stop and gasp in horror
/ cause them to throw-up
Garbage they eat at some fancy Jewish, Chinese,
Italian, Russian, European,
Indian Restaurant.
I want the crowd to be large!
I'll take the foot in my mouth and bite off each toe,
spitting them at the crowd!
I will smile to show my red-stained teeth.

I'll rip off remaining skin and hold the foot high
above my head / I'll scream in
Pain!
What's my name?
Ezell Ford, Breonna Taylor, Christian Taylor,
Charleena Lyles, Ronell Foster
When the well dressed, clean shaven, talk like all the
rest, news reporter comes to
my hospital bed / I'll tell him of my unemployment
pains, my exclusion pains, my
pains of hunger, my pains of urban exile, my thugs in
blue uniform pains, my
heart-felt, mother/father Gospel tears pains!!
I'm going to shout and sing of these pains just like
I've done so many times
before!
And, when he inquires about my foot / I'll tell him I
am in too much pain to talk
about such small things! Then, I will scream the
names of my Brothers and Sisters

Who's lives we must never forget!!
Remember their names:
Darnisha Harris, Yvette Smith, Bettie Jones
Remember their names:
Keith Childress Jr., Miguel Espinal, Jamar Clark
Remember their names:
Shantel Davis, Malissa Williams, Shereese Francis,
Remember their names:
Miles Hall, Terence Crutcher, Paul O'Neal
They, and countless others, are our documented
proof that we have experienced,
first -hand, the painful presence of pain far too
long!
Solution?
Revolution!!
Forward Ever!! Backward Never!!

Rev. Dr. Nathaniel Gadsden, is founder of Nathaniel Gadsden's Writers Wordshop and Pastor of Imani Redeemed Christian Church of God, Harrisburg, PA. He is a certified Life Coach and a Mentor for The Program: It's About Change, which works with individuals returning home from prison. He is a Staff Chaplain with UPMC Pinnacle Hospitals. He is also an Instructor with The University of Pittsburgh's Child Welfare Resource Center, and Harrisburg Area Community College. Rev. Gadsden and his wife, Patricia, co-host a weekly television show called "Life Esteem" on WHP-TV 21 (a CBS affiliate). He also is Host of the Nate Gadsden Show on Facebook Live, The Voice 17104, Harrisburg, PA.

I Can See Myself Dancing
Gwendolyn Holland

I can see myself dancing amongst the clouds
Performing for my Lord and Savior Jesus Christ

I can see myself so clearly,
Having the confidence of knowing that God is so
near and dear to me.

I can see myself turning around and around like an
Angel doing an informal ballet
As the music flows so gracefully right through my
very being
And God's pleasing eyes look down at me and say in a
soft, tender voice
"You are my dancing child so humble, meek and mild."

I can see myself dancing again and again
For it is something that I enjoyed doing
Since I was a little girl, and now that I am an adult,
Yes! I will dance for the world.

I can see myself dancing.

Love
Gwendolyn Holland

Love travels the universe and finds its way to
far off distances that we never knew existed

Love has light that forever shines
We should never want to close its blinds

Love if we acknowledge its warmth and beauty
We can still appreciate it when we are feeling moody

Love radiates beyond our imagination for it is the
source of
Healing when we are feeling at our worst

Love hungers for food and thirst for water
It too has to fill its desires
If just for a little while

Love is God in me, God in you and that love should
never die
For love reaches far beyond the sky
Love is God for he is the source

Be Encouraged
Gwendolyn Brown-Benson

This poem is written for you
I pray that God will take care of you,
Give you peace in the mist of the storm.
When you are feeling blue and don't know what to
do,
Call on Jesus and he will help you through.
I pray that when you need him the most,
You will open your heard to a forgiving God,
One who can do all the healing,
Regardless, to how you are feeling.
You are still here for a reason
In this season, You belong to me,
I have great things for you to do,
Therefore you must stay
For another day.
The road to recovery can be rough,
Nevertheless, please put your trust in God,
And he will make you tough
Because he is capable of such.
Have faith in your family and for those who care,
And most of all have faith in God,
For He saw favor in you
So be strong,
And you can't go wrong.
Cast all your burdens upon the Lord and please...
Be Encouraged

The Sky
Gwendolyn Brown-Holland

When I look at the sky so blue,
I know that God's love is very true.
You see I need his love each day,
But at times I need it more when I am feeling gray

And when I see the morning light, I need not ask
why,
For I know that God has granted me another day,
and I pray
He grants me many more until I am old and gray.

When the clouds dominates the sky,
It is usually a sign that bad weather is about to
appear
And so we take cover.
When we have bad experiences in our lives,
Please know that Jesus is near
For in him we are discovered.

Have you ever been up there in the sky,
So high above the clouds?
And looked at the beauty that they possess.
Clouds of white and blue colors,
Shapes of mountains, hills and valleys.
And if you look closely you may even see an image of
a beautiful stallion,

Or an angel with it's wings spread over the heavens.

The sky, the stairways to heaven it sometimes
seems,
But not in this time of being.
We can view the sky from the earth's girth,
Perhaps one day when Jesus comes
And we all leave this earth,
We can experience a complete view of all it's worth.

A Reflection of My Mother in Me
Gwendolyn Brown-Holland

Thank you, mother, for the love you gave to me
For when I look in the mirror, I see the reflections
of you in me
I remember all the good deeds that you portrayed
I saw your kind heart even when you were in dismay
I see you in me mother, I see me in you mother
These words I am loving to utter
The presence of your warm heart I can still feel
For I knew that it was for real
You gave me a sense of understand of my well being
And whom I needed to call on in my in my despair
which is Jesus
Because he is the one who will make my life complete
Mother I miss you so much because you were so kind
to me
The thought of you being in heaven truly sets my
mind at ease.

Gwendolyn Holland Is a poet and praise & worship dancer, born and raised in Harrisburg, PA. Gwendolyn is a member of Mt. Calvary Church of God In Christ. She has appeared in many stage productions, two of which were produced by Nathaniel Gadsden's Writers Wordshop. She is a community activist and arts educator who has worked extensively with persons of all ages. Gwendolyn attended William Penn High School and Harrisburg Area Community College.

This is an account of a true story, told in Pidgin.

A NATIVE STORY IN A NATIVE DIALECT

Winde! Washington-Nnochirionye

I saw him... I saw him in the heat, not just heat but the hellacious heat of the Lagos sun on Oshodi Road. Between Apapa to Ibadan coming from Festac to the third mainland bridge. Conductors weaving through cars on mobile morgues- vans turned into buses, doors removed to accommodate additional passengers or victims as we call them in my village. Traffic for as far as the eye can see. We no get traffic lights and stop signs. This one is every man for self, shah. See, I may be new to this land, but I no be JJC. I no be Johnny Just Come. I am a native to this village. They say I be Oigbo- White, because am American, Yoruba have even called me Tokumbo- like saying I have returned...

There was this man. He was just there. Not just standing there you understand? Ah ahh... this one, he was dead. The driver-whey see him first says, "Auntie Look away." I can't. I no fit look away. My eyes fix in his direction. Now me-o, I've neva seen a dead man. I have seen a man that has passed away- but this man was lying on the street, dead. His body dey dusty. He was covered in the hot dry Nigerian dust like Earth to Earth. And the cars- ha- the cars, they just keep going. And de people (sucks teeth) they keep moving too.

Ah ah... how come now? The driver makes the sign of the cross. I can only say, in my native, native tongue, "Oh my God!" forgetting that my main goal is to be less of me and more of them. In Pidgin English, I translate. "My God" I try Igbo on for size, "Chineke!" and I dash in a little more pidgin, my new native tongue... "God's pikeen no fit find honor -o." God's children will never find honor.

My eyes go back to the man- the dead man, shah...I don't' know him, this one I no sabe but I know he is our brother. He is a son, a friend, maybe a husband or a father. You understand? Ah-ahh. Driver, I say- "What kind of thing is this? See, eh, in my village," ehn? "you can't just leave him there. You must take him to the hospital."

"No Auntie, ah beg, I no go 'gree." he says "Now, this wahalla no be ours today."

I say to him, "In my village-eh, wahalla/ trouble be just that... trouble. And if my brother or sister get wahalla- then I get wahalla self." The driver no fit listen- he won't listen. Een no go gree. He won't agree.

The next day, riding down Oshodi Road to Ikoyi Island, they are all there. Women in bright colors with wrappas and lace and Jesus of Nazareth Sandals walking in Jesus of Nazareth dust and heat. Some dressed for work, Children in school uniforms. They move robotically and methodically to an unheard rhythm that you can only see. Babies on backs and children chasing closely behind women with their fare on platters balanced on their heads. "Pure Water!" Pure water! the women yell. A child says, "Auntie, make I bring you oranges" and makes a sign to beg for money. I buy the water- packaged in sandwich sized plastic bags. I know it's not pure and I'm not sure it's water- am certain this is on the CDC list of things NOT to consume. But I am home. I am as Nigerian as they come- I am Nkechinyere- a gift God has given, gapped teeth, coarse hair and a village in my heart- and my heart in my village. I buy the oranges in the bag and a roasted ear of corn with the roasted coconut. Na me-o, I don't even like coconut- self but the scent of the corn and the fruit, and the earth, and what must be God has me mesmerized, hypnotized, captivated and awestruck.

I say, "Driver, I no fit be late for work shah, I go wakka faster than this car. I beg, drive now." we drive and the driver says, "Auntie, Wale window. Close the window!" I wale, I wale, I close the window. He is Yoruba- from his language and his tribal marks.

He is beautiful but aromatically incorrect- I no fit wale window but shah- I no get time for wahalla this morning.

And then I see him, I see am and he is even dustier, and no less dead than he was yesterday. I forget my new language and I cry for him in de sweetest language I know, "Jesus" I mean, "Chineke." I fit tire for this language barrier.o The driver also translates, Baba. Baba-o, I hear him say in Yuroba.

On the third day, I dey search for am, shah. The man, he is gone- o. His body no longer adorns the dusty Oshodi Street. Men and women continue to vend their wares. The conductors standing on the vans slash buses whey the door dey removed, yell street names and transfer points like a song or a chant- Badagry, Oju Elegba, Ikorodu, Ikeja! The street is so packed, you no sabe if you fit move or you dey stand still you understand? People dey move with traffic like cars... cars dey roll by like people. Today, shah, I no fit chop oranges or drink pure water. I beg, make me see suya and moin-moin, and the little girl with the pretty teeth that begs for money. Today, shah, make am bring sweet fresh mangoes whey de juice dey run down arm-o. Today, just one more day- I no fit see "Uncle", the name I go call the dead brother when he comes to mind...

How come? I ask myself. How I go be big boss or "Oga" with a driver and security? And how I dey do Madame with big gele tied on my head but I no fit save people? When I dey see man where lay for street dead, I dey see him in my village tongue. English no get words for this one. America no fit allow such things. You see eh? This one now lie down for street and then die... Here, in America, we go die first and then wakka from place to place. Same reaction-o... the cars go drive by-o and de people, dey fit cover face and cross street-o... the stench of life sometimes be just like the stench of death. Wale window be like wale eyes-wale mind- wale ears-wale heart, close them all. Auntie, look away. I no get time for this kind of wahalla... In America, we go say, "Ain't nobody got time for that!" How come o? Since when we go let man die for road? What happened in this village where we no see fit for save man, eh? I beg, make I go sit with village elders. I go gist with dem and yan with dem, sit at their feet and sip knowledge or the purest water. We go break and chop sweet agege bread. We go chop suya and fried plantains or edodo while auntie makes pounded yam and foo foo... We go drink palm wine from the drinking gourd. I go ask them what happened. Where we dey go wrong? Whatin we dey do-o? What have we done? I no sabe the day where I go forget Uncle lying dead on Oshodi Road. I dey see am now. I go remember uncle in my prayers always... In my village, I go always tell this story. This Akoko. I fit say it in the language where I dey saw it. I go tell a native story in a native tongue. Maybe his story go bring back life on another road and for a different dead situation-o. One day, shah, I pray I go see Uncle in eternal life. I go greet am. This time, I go be JJC-Johnny just come, you understand? And I no sabe if God dey speak pidgin, but in my village, I go wait to hear God say, "My pikeen, my child, you dey do well well-oh. You have done well" I go think in my native-native tongue- "It wasn't easy", you understand. But I go say, "Life-eh? Now this one no be small thing-shah."

CLOUDS BEFORE FIRE AND SMOKE BEFORE RAIN

Winde! Washington-Nnochirionye

Everything in life comes with a warning sign, she said
And I've spent my life looking for signs
Searching for signs that lead to answers that I can't
see
Or questions I sometimes won't speak.
I look for signs to point out the obvious
Or at least make the truth- the answers I already
know, palatable
I search people's faces-
Finding it difficult to trust what I see, even if it
matches what I hear.
I still look for a deeper meaning
Connecting words with body language
Finding misleading mixed signals
I can't afford to miss another warning sign.
Whispering amen to cardinals in flight
Surely they have access to things on high
And she said, one day she'd be a cardinal
And though I can't be sure it's her-
I can't risk that this one may not be the answer to
the silent prayer – an unspoken hope
Her cardinal sign says something good is going to
happen
I pray daily for goodness and mercy
So I simply reply amen

A natural sky watcher from birth
I reach for the sky
Somewhere in that vast unreachable space is my limit
My goals and my angels are up there.
I watch cloud patterns and admire how God must love them.
How He baptizes them with sunlight and puts them above the rain.
I see what must be majestic presences and I wonder
Do they see me?
Big Mamma, both of my fathers, Grandma, my children, a brother, a best friend, a lover
Do they send me signs?
Do they catalog my questions?
Does Ernest still keep my secrets?
Do they deliberate and confer as a committee for my fate?
Angels perched on clouds ascending and descending.
Am I missing the warning signs?
Surely, I'd be more prepared in life instead of standing in fear of the unknown,
Feeling incomplete and void, the signs are so unclear from here.
A self-proclaimed meteorologist- I watch for weather patterns
And whether I chase the storm, or the storm chases me
The answer is always in the clouds.
And I watch them come and go

Soaking up my tears only to send them back to me, tenfold.
Does anyone see this forest I am in?
Or am I the only one looking at all of these trees?
Am I too close to the problem to see the solution?
Give me a sign.
How can you see the fire when it's raining so hard?
My life is a concoction of warning signs,
cryptograms, and mile markers.
A story of planted seeds
Indications of growth and life, evidence of struggle and sorrow-
Seasons come and gone
Hope for whatever will follow
You'd think by now I would recognize the signs
By now, I should be fluent in sign language.
I've been standing in smoke filled relationships
Waiting for the air to clear
Wondering if I'm on fire or is this relationship really burning down
Rummaging through old baggage and past heartaches
Looking for a clue of what went wrong
Hoping these bags of designer issues I've been carrying around
Will either catch on fire or at least be the fuel for the fire I've been waiting for.
Asthmatic gasps for air from the density of the smoke but I can't find fire.
Heat from all of life's problems

A burn from the weight of the world on my
shoulders
Smoke inhalations and burning are the worst ways to
die
And catastrophic ways to live
Burning within from a flame lit from love
Passionate for those things that make life
worthwhile
Emotionally combustible,
Dry roots, old relationships, unhealed hurts; kindling
for even the smallest flicker
I am a forest fire praying for the shade and cover
of whomever lingers in the clouds
Thirsty for the growth of the rain and how it
quenches my curiosities
Cleanses my thoughts and washes away my fears, my
doubts and my insecurities
If only the rain could exterminate these fires
If the smoke could dissipate, I could see my own
fires and be a fire fighter instead of a weather
woman
If the fire that burns would ignite the good in life
and spread internally from heart to heart
Instead of a community lynching- that same fire
would propel us to destinies of greatness
And I'll watch the clouds, knowing one day I too will
be there.
I'll bask in their beauty- still looking for signs of my
loved ones who watch from afar

Amen-ing at cardinals and roses blooming in off
season
Random acts of kindness and butterflies in flight will
still tickle my spirits and make me smile
Everything in life comes with a warning sign, she
said.
There is always smoke before there is fire
And there are always clouds before the rain.
Every time I stop to gaze at the clouds
Allowing my focus to shift
Something catches on fire
And when I need the rain to put out the fires
My world is filled with smoke.
Is it only my life that has clouds before the fire?
And smoke before the rain?
Or is that a missed warning sign?

WHO DO YOU SEE?

Winde! Washington-Nnochirionye

As I stand before you, in plain view and good sight,
What do you see when you look at me?
Has society defined my image or created a cultural
montage?
If you're looking, tell me, what is it you see?

From royalty and warrior bloodlines I come,
African and Native American through my skin to my
hair and in my veins.
Indigenous and aboriginal in part and somewhat
foreigner at best
For my ancestors immigrated in chains.
Who do you see?

My ancestral lineage is Biblically documented from
the beginning of time.
I'm a Motherland descendant, the product of a
slave's reality.
Our credits include the pyramids, mathematics, and
the sciences
I have a natural affinity for excellence and the
indwelling of a free man's mentality.
Who do you see?

Granddaughter to a woman, who could bear no child,
And an heiress to my father's throne.

As angels they fly freely and watch over me
So when you see me singularly, know I'm blessed and
never alone.
Who do you see?

Do you see Dante', Gibran, Shange, Maya, or
Giovanni?
Or perhaps you see one who pens her own book.
Per chance you see creativity, originality, ingenuity,
and visionary
If not focus in, my friend, take a look.
Who do you see?

Do you see sincerity and benevolence or a quiet
peaceful demeanor?
A habitation of love that's rooted in faith.
Do you see a person whom, till date, has yet to meet
a stranger?
And still believes there's hope for the human race.
Who do you see?

Now see my scars, my flaws, and imperfections.
They're medallions of honor to substantiate the
unfairness of life.
From battles fought, some won, some loss, and some
forfeited.
With my blood, sweat, and tears, a usual price.
Who do you see?

I am artist and writer a carpenter and seamstress,

Building poetic bridges and quilting a literary future
from my past
I am servant and leader and an advocate for the
defeated
A motivator and a teacher to my craft.
Who do you see?

I am Mike Brown, Trayvon Martin, Marissa
Alexander, and Kelly Williams-Bolar
I am Emmett, Nat Turner, Rosa, Garvy and Angela
too.
I am Martin, I am Malcolm, Michelle, Douglass,
Carver, and Dubois
And if you fail to see the connection, one day I'll be
you too.
Who do you see?

I speak with signs that are sacred and clandestine.
I speak with languages from many tongues and a
different land.
I speak with prudence and compassion, a universal
language to all
And I speak for diversity and the multitude of man.
Chi vede?
Qui voyez vous?
A quien ves?
Whetin' you dey see Oh?
Who do you see?

I am proud of this junction to which life has brought me.
Please take note of my poise, stature, and stance.
Through the Refiners fire, I've journeyed and will go again and again.
Not something you'll see if at first only you glance.
Who do you see?

Though my layers may seem minimal, superficial and unsophisticated,
And what your eyes see appears to be quite clear.
Seeing me with naked eyes and only your vision,
Is like having ears without listening to what you hear.
Tell me, who do you see?

This Little Light of Mine
Winde! Washington-Nnochirionye

This little light of mine, I'm going to let it shine.
This little light of mine, I'm going to let it shine.
This little light of mine, I'm going to hide it under a
basket of refuge for all I hold dear.

This light is my dreams, my creativity, my pain, my
losses, my love; returned and unreciprocated, my
anger- spent and caged, it's my hopes, my fears, my
faith, my hopeless faith, and my fearful hopes. This
light is my anxieties. My fear of rejection and of
being misunderstood.

This basket is the smile that says all is well or a
convincing cover of confidence when I'm not too sure
of myself. The basket is where I go when my trust
has been breached. It's the barrier that protects
me from heartaches and disappointments and
coincidentally, hinders me from true love and doubt-
free relationships.

My basket is the always durable, care free, and
witty, nonchalant, outspoken, and speaking out, ride
or die outer shell that you see. It's the sometimes
shy and often quite sensitive frontage that peeks
out without my permission. My basket is

simplistically complex and confusingly cumbersome. The more I hide beneath my basket; the more my light transforms and adjusts, the heavier my basket gets, and the harder it is to maintain.

One time I loved so hard, this little light of mine, it was a childhood love affair that now spans well into adulthood. With every I love you, my light got brighter. Then after years of I love you, there was never a goodbye, and now it's I still love you, and something happens to you when your S-O-U-L mate is really only an S-O-L-E mate, and somehow only your basket can protect that feeling.

On my 19 th birthday, a day to celebrate my shine, when I should have been sneaking and tiptoeing through my college sweetheart's dorm, I lost the first man I ever loved and the first man that gave me proof that he would die before his love for me would. I sat at his funeral and begged him not to leave me. He could leave the others, I swore, but if he left me there would be no need for this useless basket because without him, my light would not need to shine. His legacy became my foundation and I became a basket case.

A young girl that loses her father or loses this little light of mine before she experiences true love is a formula for failed love.

There were times when my light became intensely bright, This little light of mine.

Times I let it shine, moments and flashes of success. Friendships that last a lifetime and memories that somehow still bring laughter and smiles. And since one can never be too careful, I just keep everything under my basket and somehow, the good times and the happy moments commune with the darker ones like a proverbial melting pot.

One Christmas Eve, I sat with my Grandmother, This light of mine.

We laughed and talked for hours. Write a book, she told me. Put it all on paper.

Marry this kind of man she said. One minute, you're like Einstein, the next minute you're a Jerry Lewis poster child, she would say. That Christmas Eve, she said, don't be a Jerry Lewis poster child. Everything in life comes with warning signs, she advised. Before there's fire, there's always smoke and there are always clouds before there's rain. Don't ignore the warning signs, she forewarned. I don't know why she told me this but there was nowhere else I wanted to be on a Christmas Eve at 26 years old than hanging with my best girlfriend. She was my inspiration and my light source. She brought meaning and added wisdom to my basket and a purpose to my light.

We shared everything. She knew the complete inventory of my basket. The noble, contrite, dreadful, and the indifferent. There were no secrets- except the one she kept and tried to prepare me for that Christmas Eve. By Christmas morning, my grandmother and the light that illuminated my world were gone. I wanted to die with her, but she left too much for me to do, too much to share, too much to write.

And though it was a dim and shadowy time of my life- she continues to feed my light And selfishly, I hide that because I thought sharing her would be a betrayal to my basket and her light would eventually run out. But you just can't hide Hazel Franks. I was poster childish enough to think there wasn't enough of her light to go around. So she became a part of my basket and I hide behind her even as I share my light today.

I travelled the world and saw things that most don't see in a light-time.
I dined with the wealthiest I've ever seen. I worked for a man that for a hobby purchased a strip of the Atlantic coastline including the villages. I volunteered at an orphanage in an African village and fed fresh mangos to a healthy baby girl named Who-Knows, a shortened version of Who Knows What Tomorrow Brings. Yes, this little light of mine. She had been left to die in the darkness of a sewer, yet her survival and perseverance will always be a radiant and resplendent point of my life.

I sublet space in my basket when I cried for a man that had been lying dead for two days on a busy Nigerian road. As cars passed him by and people on foot covered their faces and crossed the street, this little light of mine dimmed and I mourned for a stranger; I prayed for his soul and still pray, till this day, that his dying will not be in vain. I visit him in my basket at my lowest points. If nothing else, I still have this little light of mine.

With each new experience, whether my light grew brighter or dim- my resolve strengthened, and my wick of life grew longer. Perhaps the opaqueness of my basket somehow thinned and somehow That which was concealed on the inside, conceivably mirrored a corrupt, unforgiving, lonely, bitter, beautifully diverse, full of surprises, and extremely perplexing world on the outside.

I put my reluctance to trust aside and allowed vulnerability to peek into my basket.
It felt safe and my basket would not mislead me- and if by chance it did, The kill switch on my light was fool proof- or at least tested by fools. I fell in love and married- for better or for worse, till death do us part. And that's how it happened- better, worse, and death, all at once. At the apex of my life, I was in love and in the next moment, I found myself putting two babies in one grave. I held and kissed my

twins one by one. And I don't know if the light extinguished or exploded, or if the basket was nailed shut with me in it. There's no darkness like a mother burying her babies and there's no basket that can camouflage or mask that kind of pain. So I cursed the light and the basket. Damn both of them!

But darkness doesn't last always.

It was after my darkest moment that my brightest, most brilliant moment came- he was healthy and for 32 weeks, he tossed and turned within me and with every pain and discomfort I cleared out space in my heart for the light-time of memories we would have. In the fall of '04, the gleam in my eye was permanently etched. My basket had a new buoyancy. This little light of mine.

Through the years, I continue to love and to live. At times, it feels like I've lost more than I've gained. It's hard to keep count in this basket.
So now, I stand before you- basket toppled upright and this little light of mine exposed.
There are scorch marks as evidence of my losses and failures and patches of spackling where I've tried to keep my secrets in.

There's a simple truth that can't be hidden. I can't hold both the basket and preserve this little light of mine at the same time.

It's either I shine in freedom or I live in darkness behind this façade.
Either I embrace the newness of what life brings or live in yesterday and gauge my decisions only by what I have kept in this basket.

It's stifling under this basket and I have a story to tell. The same basket I thought was protecting my reticence and hesitancy is now suffocating my light, this little light of mine. No more holding back my light. It can no longer be subdued by a basket. I have to let it shine - this beautiful light of mine So now my basket is ablaze. Incinerated- giving new meaning to self-combustion. Your light can only get so bright without eventually setting the basket on fire. And I think I'll let it burn! And just in case you're wondering, as my basket burns,

Just know the haze you see is forgiveness, it's the result of slow smoldering blame and guilt.
My moments of happiness, joy, and love produce an aroma of inner peace.
And the basket that once veiled that little light of mine now serves as a furnace-
Burning those things I can no longer hold, releasing billows of growth and change,
Providing fragrances of the wisdom life will bestow upon me and the memories I'll cherish for a light-time. Aromatherapy for the woman I'm becoming each day.

This little light of mine, I am going to let it shine.
That basket that once sheltered my light, let it
burn.
This little light of mine, I am going to let it shine.
Let it shine, Let it shine, Let it shine!

Heirloom Tides

Windel Washington-Nnochirionye

I've walked a million miles and crossed oceans.
I have even drowned in them.
I've lost my babies.
My tears are the high tide.
I've carried and still carry other babies on my back,
carefully tying knots to secure their dreams and
their future.
My mind plays and replays phrases and words
that I don't care to recall or maybe I have not yet
heard.
My pen moves incessantly.
My eyes are my ink and my heart is the paper.
I collect words, praying to unearth the perfect poem
for peculiar situations.
I am a Motherland experience infused with
fragmented cultures.
I am Saturday morning, hair grease and pressing
comb certified.
Big Mamma's Night Musk mixed with Catawba
Reservation red dirt
and the sounds of a summer revival provide incense
and a soundtrack for my craft.
Summers in Pontiac and sleepovers with older
cousins introduced me to pink champale, cussing, and
eyeliner; tools for some of life's most essential
moments.

I am macaroni and cheese and collard greens.
I am cassava, suya, and fu fu.
I am sushi and tiramisu.
I am the indispensable esoteric pull me up, a literary docent.
My libretto sings the songs of my ancestors,
hums the tunes of their passage, and engraves my story
in the walls of a legacy built on foundations of strength and hope.
My life is the braille of those whose shoulders I stand on.
My existence is the sign language for the voices that were silenced
and the words that were never spoken.
I am humbly gifted with a burden, so
my pen moves incessantly cataloging my testimonies of this life.
My eyes are the tear-moistened ink within a quill that never dries and never stops asking.
My heart is my paper where sentiment and words hold communion and poems are born.
Angels edit my experiences and God is my Publisher on High.
My unwritten poems are the sounds of raindrops on a tin roof,
Falling lyrically in my thoughts and dreams.
For these poems, I'll walk another million miles.
Its low tide and I labor for the birth of the poems that are happening around me.

Winde! Washington-Nnochirionye, born in Pontiac, Michigan is the daughter of Randi Massey and the Late William Howard Taft Washington and the late Lonnie "Pops" Massey. She is the proud mother of Nkemdilim Taft Nnochirionye, also a writer, artist, and Poet. Winde! has been writing since she was very young. Writing short stories, poems, and keeping journals have always been her go-to and continues to allow her to express herself through verse, stanza, and storytelling. Winde! is the author of Clouds Before Fire And Smoke Before Rain, her first publication. She is currently working on a fiction novel, "The Tempest Is Raging".

Our Moon

Taft Nnochirionye

She's a stargazer
The, "wake up at 2AM"
Stargazer
Counting the stars like
God counting the hairs on your head
And holding every twilight
I the palm of her hands
But she's a lover too
Expressing her love through astronomy
Exploring the sky
Like one would explore the mind
And the truest beauty of that
Is for a woman confined in a 365-day year
She finds it in her heart to love you with all
10,585 days in a year on Saturn
So we call it our moon
The halo is a reminder of our love for the other
And the late-night phone calls
The 2018 Bonnie and Clyde
And if that doesn't work
Try Elliot and Olivia
And every episode
Is another unseen star shining brighter than the
last?
So we call at 6 AM

We let our eyes reflect in the light and our voices
become the water
Freezing time
And saying in that moment
Traveling thousands of miles
To see that one star
And I show my love with all
60,200 days of a Neptunian year
Because for us, to the moon and back just doesn't
cut it
And then
We sit in silence
The loudest noise there will never be
We sit there searching
A face
His face
The beating of his heart
And then we become observers
And no matter how many days are in a plutonian year
Sometimes the easiest thing to see
Are the stars right before
Yeah that's my grandmother
A stargazer

White

Taft Nnochirionye

It's too early
Too damn early for me to be this angry
It's too early for the shouts to echo through the
barely woke halls
It's just too early for doors to be slammed
Hearts to be broken
And for minds to close
But yet here we are
In a whirlpool of frustration
Clawing at each other's neck
Not caring if the other bleeds out in the process
It's too early for me to be sick and tired of being
tired
But it's like I'm playing Uno with life
And they have all the best cards, hitting me left and
right
"Skip"
You're cancelled
"Reverse"
Put it back and try again
"Plus Four"
Extra stress
And God forbid it pulls a color change just as I get
the hang of that one
It isn't the time for me to withdraw all of my trust
Deposit some mixed feelings

And go on about my day
And the shouts sound like 6:40
And my tears sound like 7:30
And my regret feels like 8:20
But I try to stay strong until I feel like 6:00
It's too early for aguish to plague my mind
For envy to spread like an infection
And for anxiety to be a stomach bug
And to everything I've ever loved

I can't say I'm sorry

Because it's five in the morning
And it feels like my rainbow isn't enough
It feels like it's not worth the extra nap
If I don't plan on waking up after
But it's too early
Too early
And the early bird always gets caught in the snare

Defenestrate

Taft Nnochirionye

don't be afraid of the dark
let it creep up on you
fall into its arms
evacuate your mind
never look back
allow yourself to slip from reality
then slowly open the window
take back your fears
reluctantly remove yourself
the dark is no longer your friend
and now try to throw it out the window
for the rest of eternity

Taft Nnochirionye is a 15-year-old poet going into his senior year of high school at Susquehanna Township High School. He has attended the Writers Wordshop with his mother (Winde! Nnochirionye) for over three years. He believes that art is one of the purest forms of expression and with it, we can forge a better tomorrow.

THE WORD CAST SPELLS
Edward Daniels

TRUE HEALING ENERGY WORD OF RIGHTEOUS
DIVINE
SPLITTING ADAM
SPIRITUAL PURPOSE LOVE INITIATES TRUTH
TELLING IGNORANCE IS NO
GOOD ACTIVATING DIVINE ANSWER MANKIND
ATOM/ATUM/ATIM
ALTERING TRUTH OF MANKIND/ ALTERING
TRUE UNIVERSAL MAN/
ACTIVATING TRUTH IGNORING MANKIND
JESUS/THE CHRIST
JUSTIFING ENERGIES SOUL UNRIGHTEOUS
SPIRIT/ TRUE HEALING
ENERGY COMPASSIONATE HEALING
RIGHTEOUSNESS INITIATING
SPIRITUAL TRUTH
SIN/SON/SUN THE EYE OWE YOU SHALL SEE
SPIRIT OF NATURE/ SPIRIT UPLIFTING
NATURE/ SPIRIT IGNORING
NATURE
HELL/HEAL
HEALING ENERGY LOVING LIES/HEALING
ENERGY ACTIVATING LOVE

THE WHISPER IN THE WILDERNESS

Edward Daniels

THOUGHTS AND DESIRES/ ENVY AND
JEALOUSY
THE DIAGNOSIS OF MANKINDS DISEASE.
MENTAL ILLNESS WE
NEVER TREATED. OUT OF CONTROL SOCIETIES
TREATMENT IS
NEEDED. BOW DOWN TO MY DESIRES/DISEASE
AND CHASE A DREAM
THAT HAS KNOW END. THE ANSWER WHY?
THE INFECTION OF THE PARISITE YOU PICKED
UP IN THE WILDERNESS!
THAT PARISITE WAS DESIRES TO HAVE
IMAGES AND THINGS YOU ENVY
AND JEALOUSY CREEPS IN THROUGH
UNRIGHTEOUS ACTS. SPIRIT
IGNORING NATURE (SIN) YOUR UNDER ATTACH.
As the spirit of unrighteous has done with the
history of civilization, he has done to mankind. The
truth was scattered through-out the four corners
of the planet, making it difficult to piece together
the biggest lie ever told.

THERE IS ONLY 1 TRIBE HUMANITY SOMEONE
TOLD A LIE AND

SEPERATED THE HIVE. A BATTLE BEGINS TO
SURVIVE,

The Twelve tribes of the House of IS-REAL have
scattered throughout, The Four Corners of The
Planet. Re-Member I have walked with you! Re-Call
my Covenant.
Re-Gather my people, for you shall know me by my
word for it is written on you heart. The dark clouds
of negative rain down on you and it began to confuse
your consciousness and the light of HIM, who has
created us you could no longer see your vision and
thoughts have changed. The sons and daughters of
the Creator we were totally unprepared for the
negative environment to which you had willing
subjected yourselves, Immediately and without
warning, in the back of their minds/conscious you
began to experience the energy effects of virtual
opposites their REFLECTION. THEIR YING AND
YANG THERE LEFT AND RIGHT HEMISPHERE OF
YOUR BRAIN HAS BEEN SEPERATED.
They began to manifest symptoms of jealousy and
anger along with your pride and ego. This parasite
lays deep in the subconscious confusing our rights
and wrong for personal gain now greed follows them
for the first time the master builders of the
universe have been infected. The sons and daughters
began to investigate virtue's opposites, disregarding
the warning. Instead of removing yourselves from
the negative energy you walked further into those

thoughts! The Divine Consciousness of the sons and daughters of HIM, became overwhelmed by mental image projected from the indulgence in non-virtual thoughts, desires and actions pursuing a dream that are not yours. The Great Sun/Son, which has always been visible and shining within your consciousness, the light was blocked by walls and potholes of ignorance, you were overcome by a self-conscious state now constantly regenerated by a new dark and negative egotism supported by the accumulation of non- virtue mental images and action. Falling deeper and deeper into the desires by non-
virtues thoughts, you finally lost all vision of the body of Christ (RIGHTEOUSNESS). With this great loss of spiritual vision you lost and forgot your connect to the universe. While isolated in the negative environment the dark thoughts continued to form totally overpowering them energized by the forces of desire, the non-virtue mental images establishing a center of controlled conscious and we all have been infected.

E=MC'2 THE WORDS EYE PUT IN THE AIR OUT OF MY MOUTH
EYE SCATTER TREATMENT ABOUT. CLEAN WATER/WISDOM EYE BRING
TO NURTURE THE ROOTS FOR THE HARVEST TO BEGIN.

THE SEED OF DAVID
Edward Daniels

AS IT WAS WRITTEN FOR ALL TO SEE EYE
WROTE THE NOTE FOR YOU TO READ.
HOW EGO PRIDE AND GREED HAS INFECTED ME.
AS IT WAS WRITTEN IN THE BOOK WHEN THE
YOKE OF IRON IS REMOVED IT'S BECAUSE YOUR
MIND IS TOOK.
1619 - 2019 EYE HAVE WALK WITH YOU BUT EYE
WAS UNSEEN.
YOU WERE CAUGHT UP IN THE ILLUSSION AND
DREAM.
WHEN EYE SPOKE WITH YOU YOU DIDN'T KNOW
WHAT EYE MEAN,
WHEN EYE ASKED ABOUT CREATION YOU
DIDN'T HAVE TIME.
SO EYE WALK WITHYOU IN THE WILDERNESS
AS YOU COMMIT CRIME.
EYE WALK WITH YOU AS WE STOOD IN LINE.
LIKE CATTLE WITH KNOW MIND.
FROM THE OUT HOUSE TO THE WHITE HOUSE
EYE HAVE WALKED WITH YOU ALL.
FROM THE FIRST ORDER OF RIGHTEOUSNESS
EYE AM MAKING THIS CALL THE BLACK MAN
HAS RISEN
HE HAS BRIDGED THE GAPS
WHAT WAS TAKEN FROM YOU
EYE AM GIVEN BACK.

EYE CARRY CLEAN WATER/WISDOM
TO SPRINKLE ABOUT TO NURTURE MOOR SEEDS
TO COME OUT.
AS PROMISED, YOU Eye O U RA TURN THE
SPIRIT YOU ONCE NEW YOUR CONNECTION TO
NATURE THAT PROVIDES ALL
YOUR NEEDS,
IT WAS YOUR DECSION TO LEAVE AND STOP
SEARCHING FOR ME
EYE AM RETURNING
THE LIGHT SO YOU CAN SEE WHAT IS
WRITTEN ON YOUR HEART HAS COME FROM ME.

THE LAWS OF THE UNIVERSE
Edward Daniels

THE ONE LAW THAT SUPERSEDES ALL IF IT HURTS HARMS OR DESTROYS ANY LIVING CREATURE IT IS DEEMED UNRIGHTEOUS FIND ANOTHER WAY. DOMINION OF THE PLANET WAS FOR YOUR PROTECTION NO LONGER SHALL WE LET OTHERS DISRESPECT IT. YOU HAVE BROKEN THE LAW THE 12 JUDGES EYE CALL

THE LAWS OF THE UNIVERSE

The Law of Divine Oneness - everything is connected to everything else. What we think, say, do and believe will have a corresponding effect on others and the universe around us.

Law of Vibration - Everything in the Universe moves, vibrates, and travels in circular patterns, the same principles of vibration in the physical world apply to our thoughts, feelings, desires, and wills in the Etheric world. Each sound, thing, and even thought has its own vibrational frequency, unique unto itself.

Law of Action - Must be employed in order for us to manifest things on earth. We must engage in actions that supports our thoughts dreams, emotions, and words

Law of Correspondence - This Universal Law states that the principles or laws of physics that explain the physical world energy, Light, vibration, and motion have their corresponding principles in the etheric or universe "As above, so below"

Law of Cause and Effect - Nothing happens by chance or outside the Universal Laws... Every Action (including thought) has a reaction or consequence" We reap what we sow"

Law of Compensation- The Universal Law is the Law of Cause and effect applied to blessings and abundance that are provided for us. The visible effects of our deeds are given to us in gifts, money, inheritances, friendships, and blessings.

Law of Attraction - Demonstrates how we create the things, events and people that come into our lives Our thoughts, feelings, words, and actions produce energies which, in turn attract like energies. Negative energies attract negative energies and positive energies attract positive energies.

The Law of Perpetual Transmutation of Energy - All persons have within them the power to change the conditions of their lives. Higher vibrations consume and transform lower ones; thus, each of us can change the energies in our lives by understanding the Universal Laws and applying the principles in such a way as to effect change

Law of Relativity - Each person will receive as series of problems (Tests of Initiation/Lessons) for the purpose of strengthening the light within each of these tests/lessons to be a challenge and remain connected to our hearts when proceeding to solve the problems. This law also teaches us to compare our problems to others problem into its proper perspective. No matter how bad we perceive our situation to be, there is always someone who is in a worse position. It's all relative.

Law of Polarity - Everything is on a continuum and has and opposite. We can suppress and transform undesirable thoughts by concentrating on the opposite pole. It is the law of mental vibrations.

Law of Rhythm - Everything vibrates and moves to certain rhythms... These rhythms establish seasons, cycles, stages of development, and patterns. Each cycle reflects the regularity of God's Universe. Masters know how to rise above negative parts of a cycle by never getting to excited or allowing negative things to penetrate their consciousness.

<u>Law of Gender</u> - The law of gender manifests in all things as masculine and feminine. It is this law that governs what we know as creation. The law of gender manifests in the animal kingdom as sex. This law decrees everything in nature is both male and female. Both are required for life to exist.

Jesus is Tested in the Wilderness
Edward Daniels

BLACKMAN Is Tested in the Wilderness
Then BLACKMAN was led by the Spirit into
the wilderness to be tempted [a] by
the devil. After wondering forty years and forty
nights, he was hungry. The
tempter came to him and said, "If you are the Son
of God, tell these stones
to become bread/money."

Jesus answered, "It is written: 'Man shall not live on
bread/money alone, but
on every word that comes from the mouth of God."

Then the devil took him to the holy city and had him
stand on the highest
point of the temple. "If you are the Son of God," he
said, "throw yourself
down. For it is written:

"'He will command his angels concerning you,
 and they will lift you up in their hands,
 so that you will not strike your foot against a
stone."

Blackman answered him, "It is also written: 'Do not put the Lord your God to the test.' " Law of Relativity - Each person will receive as series of problems (Tests of Initiation/Lessons) for the purpose of strengthening the
light within each of these tests/lessons to be a challenge and remain
connected to our hearts when proceeding to solve the problems. This law
also teaches us to compare our problems to others problem into its proper
perspective. No matter how bad we perceive our situation to be, there is
always someone who is in a worse position. It's all relative.

Again, the devil took him to a very high mountain and showed him all the
kingdoms of the world and their splendor. "All this I will give you," he said,
"if you will bow down and worship me." EGO, PRIDE AND GREED

Jesus said to him, "Away from me, Satan (SPIRIT ALTERING TRUTH AND
NATURE)! SPIRIT IGNORING NATURE (SIN) For it is written: 'Worship the
Lord your God and serve him only. SPIRIT OF NATURE(SON) IS MAKING

THIS CALL, EYE AM WALKING WITH THE SPIRIT
UPLIFTING NATURE(SUN)
EYE AM CARRING THE WATER/WISDOM TO
AWAKE YA!

Then the devil (Destroy energies value-initiated
lies) and closed your third
eye but when the light came darkness left him, and
angels came and
attended him. TELESTAI

Edward Daniels Jr. Born on the 8 month and 3rd day
1961. Born from the fertility of Taurus the bull Lucy
Virginia Woods, born and raised in Middletown. Then
attended Lincoln University graduate of the class of
83.30 years working corporate America. Then wrote and
designed medical billing and coding curriculums and
facilitated as well. Analyzing date and statistical
reviews. Facilitator of programs, motivational speaker,
inspires others to read. A griot, cohosted talk radio show
discussing sports culture, race and politics. An
entrepreneur currently working on 2 books, Blackmans
Mental State in America and The Academy of Higher
Conscious and The Journey of a Seed.

Life Matters

Maria James-Thiaw

First, Treyvon.
A rainbow in his pocket,
A hood on his head.
Smashed into concrete like
little more than a bug.
Shot dead on a snack run.

That first awakened the deep black fear,
that griping cramp that hurts so far down
you know your ancestors feel it too.

Then Michael,
left laid out, lifeless,
blood puddle seeping
into gravel, mixing with earth,
painting a picture of Black crimson rage.

Then Freddy in Mobtown,
fires clawing through concrete
for life snuffed out.

Then the coverage of
the black man they
climbed like a mountain,
A white arm locked like a bear claw
around his throat,

Squeezing, squeezing, squeezing till
blue lips spit out words, small. Final.
I. Can't. Breathe.

Then, a new tool, Facebook Live
shows Officer Shaky Hands
killing Castille in his car.
Next day, Alton Sterling is dead.
Lurking emojis turn red.

Then, signs signal danger-
Educated Black Woman,
 Sandra Bland, on route to university.
Her mind, sharp as a weapon.
Her tongue, a wick that could
not be extinguished-
Not without a noose.

Then, George's dead mama came to
meet him as he was pressed
into concrete for nearly nine minutes.
He pushed out those three familiar words
Three earth shaking, world changing words:
I. Can't. Breathe.

Millions mask up and put
feet to pavement
but still, the karens call.

Help! Black man walking.

Walking through the blackest of nights,
Elijah seemed "suspicious." Deemed dangerous.
His mask was a hug that
helped him face the world.
Another snack run ends tragically.

Then, so many more, hung like rocks
'round our necks in blue ocean.
Our breath borrowed, like time.
We woke, wary of the very air.
I'm just different, Elijah pleaded.
I'm just different, that's all!

When your child's needs are special,
 It gets heavier. Pulls you lower.
Each story adds weight
to the knee on your neck.

Now Miami,
23-year-old sits wide open
playing with noncompliance.
 His mental health worker, Black,
lay bleeding beside him, hands up.
Don't. shoot.
And the cop said he
didn't mean to fire at the caretaker,
didn't mean to steal our breath again,
didn't want to be another blue headline.

He was aiming for the other one.

Nonverbal, misunderstood,
Toy truck in hand.
I'm just different. I'm different, that's all.

When your child's needs are special
The weight gets heavier, but
Their lives matter, too.

Solidarity
Maria James-Thiaw

Today, the white supremacist out my window
is taking a harassment break.
He won't stare at my children, or
run to the nearest Trump flag flyer
to share his poison about us.
He isn't shaking his fist in my direction,
or throwing me that practiced skinhead glare.

According to his page, today's focus is our
common enemy – chronic pain!
Clearly this could be a crumb.
A way to steer 105 of my wokest-woke
white friends off the scent of his racist rants.
a way to confuse the social media police
with their 'community standards;'
a way to keep Black acronyms off his doorstep.

Today, on Juneteenth, in the middle of a revolution
BLM aren't terrorists or racists to him.
Today the message is plain. This white boy's in pain--
  And I get it.

The rainbow-colored words appeared to grow
out of my grass despite him.
 "In this house, we believe
Kindness is first, Black Lives Matter, Love is Love..."

And there he stood, flared up like a firework in
July
The clenched fists, the redness rising from chin up
over
the skin of his exposed scalp.

Oh, how it churned in his belly
when someone shared his post with me,
The 'loudmouth black racist' with her 'BLM sign'
He was crippled under the anvils of my voice, as it
thrust its discontent into his yard,
with a hearty full caps curse.

And two by two anti-racists all day
came to sit on my lawn. Peacefully. In community.

The white supremacist out my window
Attacked online on Juneteenth, amidst
A revolution and got so worked up that
Today his gnarled joints can't even lift a finger
to post a mean meme.
His nerves burn like crosses on each vertebra.

Rest well, nemesis. Wrap up in an old
Red white and blue blanket of privilege,
Or maybe your daddy's white robe.
Sink deep into nightmares of the
2050 demographic change.
Close your eyes to the
blinding glow of

Black excellence and beloved community
that sits in unity
on the other side of the street.

CoVid Haiku

Maria James-Thiaw

My poem-bone healed.
Now catharsis can begin.
Seven days shut in.

Going Gently

Maria James-Thiaw

The day I thought I was dying
I decided to
carefully fold up my somedays,
keep them tucked in a trunk
in a cobweb-laced corner of a dark attic—
The kind of place where you put
things unfinished,
things that were never meant to be.

The day I thought I was dying
I tried
to tug tightly closed divine doors open,
searched the web but couldn't see myself,
felt Dylan's judgmental gaze
burned into my back.
I knew what he thought of weary me,
accepting fatigue,
wearing that good night like a blanket,
too afraid to rage.

The day I thought I was dying
I chose
someone to haunt –
not to scare, but follow, and
leave whispers like little gifts.
I'd be his cool breeze and his

'something told me,'
the song incessantly singing
in his head.

The day I thought I was dying
I searched for a bucket
to hold my will-dos.
Tears formed and fell like wasted time,
clocks melted and slid off my cheeks
streaming into shaky hands
My mind flipped through mental pictures
of my boys,
and the man who may not be
Mother enough for them.

I raged. I finally raged.
I chose not to go gently.
My light flickers, but the candle still burns.

Maria James-Thiaw is the author of 3 collections of
poetry and a performance poet living in Central PA.
She is the author of the 2018 hit choreopoem,
Reclaiming My Time: An American Griot Project
and Sankofa's *Bridge the Gap,* which she co-wrote
with Sharia Benn. She is in charge of Creative
Writing at the Capital Area School of the Arts and
has 15 years of experience teaching on the college
level. In 2018 she formed a nonprofit called Reclaim
Artist Collective aimed at bringing affordable arts
programs to groups in marginalized areas.
Www.ReclaimArts.org

Faith

Keyontay Ricks

The lord is the artist, earth is the canvas, he's the
one that drew the mountains,

Then he informed us in his word that faith moves
the mountains,

This means that no one can have true faith, without
x-ray vision, if they cannot see through the
mountains,

Understand a lack of faith is responsible for giving
power to the mountains,

we will face mountains until the lords says it's our
time to depart, for our only true mountains exist in
our mind which defined as our heart,

You must understand the artist, before you can
understand the art,

In his image he designed mankind,
Many of us have not Walked by faith we walked by
sight,

based upon past decisions, we would have been
better off blind,

Study the basic instructions before leaving earth,
Apply instruction and obtain your success,

Excuses are useless, if you don't apply the basic
instructions before leaving earth, you will
foolishly fail this (opened book test).

We are not of this world, so don't be led by the
flesh,

Your score does not need to reflect 100% as long as
you strive your hardest, and do your best,

You were not designed to fit in with the crowd,
You were uniquely designed to stand out,

Before we were born in the flesh, our lives were
planned out,

Free will gives us the choice to comply with the
instruction or go against,

Just remember that faith, and worry does not exist
on the same side of the fence,

Keep your faith, feed your faith, allow it to expand,

Faith moves mountains so the only thing we need to
vision when we walk with the lord is flat land.

Cariol Law
Keyontay Ricks

Permanent suspension, plus they took her pension,
the serious crime that Cariol Hallthorn committed
was that she stopped white officers from using
their hands as the rope for the modern-day
lynching, of a Blackman.

Yes, penalized for standing up to save a brother,
because not only was she an honorable police officer,
like many others Cariol Halthorn horn is a mother.

She did not turn her back on police misconduct, she
did not ignore the facts and just leave, She
responded when another George floyd being choked
by police said " I can't breathe ",

Cariol actions prevented a tragic death, thanks to
Cariol this Blackman is very fortunate to take
another breath, she stood for what was right, it
backfired in her face and exploded, instead of being
fired for what she prevented from happening, she
should have been rewarded, she should have been
promoted.

That speaks a lot for the leadership of the police
department, also shedding light on community
leaders that supported cariol's penalty,

She saved an innocent Black life from being taken, and for doing so Cariol horn became public enemy,

She was sued by the department, and hated by the police, if the leaders in our justice system perceive saving a black man's life as being wrong, that suggest that it would have been right if she turned her back and the black man ended up deceased,

It's sad, that they were not glad, that she stood up and saved the life of a man,
Divided we fall, they would rather that we fall, but together we will stand,

We stand, together we stand against lynching it does not matter whether it results from a rope or a hand.

We stand for justice with Cariol, it's time that we unite.

This is not just about Black or White, it's about exposing what's wrong and supporting what is right.

Let's honor Cariol for the courageous thing she has done,

Be mindful that Cariol past actions saved a mother's son,

When George Floyd screamed for mom, it superseded nationalities, religions, and different skin colors,

George Floyd's scream was a scream calling out to all mothers.

The system is demonic, the truth is so clear, he
If one of the officers present with George Floyd,
Would have had cariols courage, George Floyd would still be here,

That could have been your baby, with the police kneeling on his neck, for what our sister prevented from happening, she deserves her pension, recognition, honor and respect.

What she did was correct,

My people I humble ask,
I humble ask
That we share this message,
Assist our sister,
And support Cariols Law being passed.
This mother stood up and demand that Cariol's law is passed

To be free

Keyontay Ricks

Perceptions will change,
as knowledge you gain,
Watch it, read it, or hear it,
Confidence affects performance, but love is the
medicine that heals the flesh, the mind, and the
spirit,
Forgiveness is for self,
unforgiveness is toxic to health,
hatred is a poison that's vicious,
But knowledge is power,
cherish every second, minute, and hour,
mental wealth supersede material riches,
Tired of hurting Obstacles are certain, continue
working until obtaining what you seek,
7 days can't be your attitude when self-reflecting,
this means that you are not (week) weak,
Uniquely designed,
to stand out and shine,
you are a child of the most high,
Limitations are mental plantations,
we are limitless as the sky,
so fly little bird fly,
allow your eagle wings to soar,
go beyond and above,
continue to lead by love,
This is what you were created for,
To be free

All Lives Matter

Keyontay Ricks

Black life's matter, white life's matter, all life's matter to the creator,

Jesus did not mention a religious title when he informed us that we should love our neighbor.

Feeding into racism is like giving labor, giving birth to Satan's child.

Racism is ignorance that causes division among the crowd.

Starve the beast of racism don't entertain the frivolous chatter,

In God's eyes Black life matters, white life's matter all life matters.

Everyone is severely broken as the glasses of justice continue to shatter,

Positive Change will only become a reality if Together we climb this ladder,

Ladder of success, overcome your flesh, it's Satan we have seen the proof,

Understand that Time reveals all hidden truth, for American is a house that really needs a roof, new walls, new floors, complete reconstruction, even though we all know the foundation was built on corruption,

Things don't happen overnight, together we need to stand for what's right, be persistent, passionate, and patient,

America has never been good, because the same demonic system has always been in place controlling our nation.

Black life's matter, white life's matter, all life's matter to God.

Police brutality sponsored by taxpayer's salary statistics expose the facade,

They kill blacks and whites, violate our rights, google the number of people killed by police in past years it's sad,

Google the wrongful imprisonment, the malicious prosecutions, the whole demonic system is bad,

Wrongful incarcerations, decades on prison plantations, black whites, everyone gets treated like trash,

This happens to blacks & Latinos more, also to whites that's poor, a different standard of justice applies to the lower class.

Lord we pray that one day, we can truly say that we are free at last,
 striving to gather the pieces because we are all broken like a glass,

It's destined to crash, The system has been masked, with white sheets and a burning cross,

Let's focus on our future and not continue to be stagnated by everything we has lost,

Divided we fall but together we stand, together we unite and speak,

together we vote and no one gets elected unless they agree to support the changes we seek.

The mayor, the president, all representatives including the district attorney,

For we are the people, we have the power, together we must be led by Love, in the future as we take this journey.

We all have one heart, on brain, one soul, one life, the great I am that I am, has made us equal,

No one is less or greater, color don't matter we are all Gods people,

For God is love, and anything that does not coincide with love is evil,

Forgive by never forget not long-ago slavery was and in some ways it's still legal,

However, the darkness of the world cannot override the light,
Continue to shine, that's why they called you sunshine you shine so bright,

For the sun gives life to the earth, all negativity should be restricted,

Earth is a temporary residence for us all, from which one day we will be evicted,

Don't be conformed to this world, be transformed by the renewing of your mind,

Let's come together bonded in love and in the
presents of this darkness shine,

Black life's matter, white life's matter, all life's
matter, all the time,

This is not about black and white; it's about changing
what's wrong and standing for what's right

Together let's hold the sign,
Because all lives matter all lives matter no one is
less or greater,
In Crist name I pray for a supernatural healing from
the creator,
I pray from every family and person that has been
truly broken,

I pray that all the deceased, can Rest In Peace,
I pray that the gates of heaven are opened,
In God's eyes we are equal, we are not less or
greater,

Black lives matter, white lives matter, all lives
matter to the Creator,

Reality

Keyontay Ricks

Such a beautiful race,
Smiles disguised frowns from the sad face,
Of our broken people,
Viewed as 3/4 of man,
We have never been treated equal,
Taken from the motherland,
Enslaved to serve another man
On a plantation,
And still Treated as if we did not build this nation,
Wrongful incarceration,
Less than an animal the vision us,
Mentally, physically, financially,
They have imprisoned us,
They have raped and abused our daughters sisters
and mothers,
They have hung, torched, killed, our sons, fathers,
uncles, and brothers.
This is not about skin color being dark or light,
black, brown or white,
This is about exposing what's wrong and standing for
what's right.
I don't encourage being violent,
But is time that we stand together and stop being
silent,
Unite stand for what's right we are all sisters and
brothers,

All of these children from police brutality were taken from their father and mothers,
All of the fathers and mothers police killed
Left parentless children behind,
Stop acting as if your blind,
Broken youth, exposing truth,
We shall not ignore,
This is a spiritual war,
And I ask the troops, what are you really fighting for?
I thought the military served the country and stood for America's protection.
Our people nonviolently protest, and snipers have guns Aimed in their direction.
The problem is that the police keep killing the people that they should be protecting.
So when the troops are deployed
Just understand that every picture is a picture of a life,
And a future that the police have destroyed.
This is reality.

Keyontay Ricks is an exoneree from Buffalo, New York. He is a creative artist who shares his life experiences through poetry, music, and books. He is a motivational speaker who is dedicated to empowering others spiritually mentally, physically, and financially. You can view works on Facebook, Instagram, sound cloud, and YouTube under Keyontay Ricks.

It's not you it's me

Terri D.

It's not you it's me
I've lost count on how many times I've heard these
words spoken to me
After so many times hearing the same line, one
starts to wonder
 Is it really you or is it really me?

If it's not me then why is it that I keep hearing
these same words
Spoken from different men time and time again
What is the reason I keep ending up in the same old
place?
Time after time giving my all just to get the same
line thrown in my face
The heavy sigh then the coined phrase. Baby's it's
not you it's me
Well you see after hearing these words enough
times it finally
Starts to sink in.
You and all the men before you who have spoken
these words to me were right
It isn't you it's me

I am the one who deserves the love I have been
giving you

It's not you it's me that deserves the beauty of finding the one love
Who knows how to give and receive love
It's not you it's me who deserves that special someone who recognizes how very special I am
The beauty the lies within me

The words you always say to me
It's not you it's me

I never thought I would be the one saying those words
I've often heard them from others when they were trying to explain away some hurt, they were about to dish out
All along it was me not them who should have been saying it's not you it's me
It's me who deserves to be treated like the real woman I am
Not just some piece of trash you can discard
Why do I try so damned hard to make you want me? Love me?
When all along I should have seen that it's not you it's me who deserves the love that I have to give.

It's not you it's me who has finally seen the light
I am going to be alright
You can take your excuse and move along because I am done with all of you losers
I finally have figured out that it's not YOU it's ME

The way you...

Terri D.

I wake up each morning to the reality that
I am blessed to see another day but yet
You're still not here and I am not there
As the days, turn into months and it's soon going to
be a year
What I fear most is fading memories
Of the things I don't want to forget
Our first kiss
The way you looked at me on our wedding day.
The way you fought for me that day when I tried to
leave
The way you have fought for me every day since
The way you reach for me to pull me closer in your
sleep
The way you whistle when you arrive to get my
attention
The way you protect me from everything except the
things I am deathly afraid of.
The way you let me see you in a way no one else does
The way you said you'd wait for me and you have.
The way you are everything I need you to be.

Feeling You
Terri D.

You say slow and steady
Cause you are not quite ready
To let yourself go and let your feelings flow freely
Babe listen close and hear me
When I say to you that

I'm feeling you
Our connection is so intense
It feels heaven sent
I prayed to God for a man who
Could stimulate my mind
I don't want to waste any more time
I prayed to God for a spiritual man
God has a plan
Two souls so far apart
Our paths crossed
A subconscious spark
Ignited verbal communication
Where we would discover each other's inner beauty
Character, substance
Our common threads
Babe you are in my head
Slowly and steadily moving downward into my heart
Before we part, I need to know
Can you let your guard down?
And let your feelings flow freely

Babe listen close and hear me
I'm feeling you
Let go and feel me too

Terri Martinez is a blogger and author who writes under the pen name Terri D. She published her debut novel titled Yesterday's Lies in 2011. Terri has since released four more novels and had a poem published as part of an anthology of poems about love titled Bubblin' Brown Sugar. Terri also published a memoir titled, Passport Wife and two Journaling books, Journaling for Self-Care for Young Adults and Journaling for Self-Care for persons in Recovery. Terri has another novel titled Love, Lies and Fight scheduled for release in the fall of 2020.

Young Dark Brown Sugar Diva

Roe Braddy

Her head was downcast for a while, they said her
hue was too dark, she couldn't qualify
She didn't rate
They put her down,
They wouldn't let her in,
Won't let her join the fight, nor the fun
This is what they said about her kind of black. You
know, too black to bring any good,
Too black, like the neighbor's black cat that brought
bad luck to your doorstep
Blackballed and put out on the street like an old
worn sofa left for Thursday's trash pickup
In the midst of the blackout we ran thru the street
finding our way lost, once again we were in the bad
dark, not the good light This was our kind of black,
the black that we knew so well
But today's black, that's a different kinda black,
kinky coily black,
Melanin poppin' like fried chicken in a black cast iron
skillet all of us rising up and getting in your nostrils
That kinda black
Queen of hearts and Jack of spades, but then came
along blackjack

We hit the nail on the head, now the juice of our
kind of black is sweeter than the berry of
Disappointment, segregation and deportation
Angela Davis stood proud and fought, jailed and
labeled for this kind of black
Antwan Rose and fell on the street of Steel
Rodney asked, "Why can't we all just get along?"
Dr. King just wanted us to make it to the mountain
top
This is our kind of black
Beautiful black baby girls wanna know, "Why am I so
black? Stand up tall, hold up your head with it's
Kinky crown Don't let them tell you that your black is
the bad kinda black, don't let them tell you that your
skin doesn't hold a magical glow
Don't let them tell you that you'll never reach your
goal
Hold up your head little brown sugar diva

You ride on the back of your forefathers who were
strong ebony people who wore the scars of
disappointment, strife and undeserved imprisonment
Your lineage is one of noble character and refined
endurance
We need you to guard up your loins for the fight,
the fight that only you have the strength to see us

all through, this strength comes from your kind of black
You have been passed the scepter that was held by Egypt's royal priestess
 The daughter of the most- high king
You are a child of God known since the beginning of the earth's existence
Knit in your mother's womb waiting to blossom into your fullness
You are made in his image, beautifully and fearfully
 in fact, fierce,
This is your kind of black

I am Positive of This

Roe Braddy

Dammit, that good for nothing bastard. I should have known it, there were signs. My girls told me that I married wrong. My own momma told me that I could do better and that I had settled. Settled, I was trying to settle, settle myself down with who I though was gonna be my forever. Now my forever, done given me this thing, this dreaded thing, I won't name it. Because it is forever. No, I won't dignify it with a name. They said he wasn't nothing but a player. He played me alright, just like a damn fiddle. Problem is, I still love him right down to the marrow of my bones. This thing that haunts me nights, giving me the sweats.

Causing me to give over my spirit to hate the very core of my being. Don't judge me, don't give me your stink eye. You would have loved him too. I remember the day that my eyes were laid upon him. Yes, I wasn't looking, it was like a cattle prod, a hot poker that I couldn't resist. I was branded with his name written right here. (Pats her chest) Go on now girl, go get that sweet, black thang. Pushed real hard up against his smooth talking and wayward ways. I was trapped, I couldn't move. He took away my fight.

I know what you are thinking, she's a damn pushover. I'm not. I used to think that I would settle down with a guy who had and KEPT a white-collar job, you know a nine to five. Well, hell, half the men in my neighborhood are on the pipe or in a 6 by 8. He was long, black and bold. Told me things about myself that made me stand up tall, like a black woman who had places to go. Made me feel like I was somebody, who was going to places way beyond this little hell hole of a town. I was going places, I should have kept it moving, but no I looked back. Me and Lot's wife. Salt would be a blessing about now. It does make me a bit more than a little salty.

Two of my girls wanted to come with me today, but I told them that I needed to go alone, it needed to sink in. POSITIVE. I am positive that I got a six-year-old son that I gotta get to daycare tomorrow. I am positive that I gotta take my black behind to work so I can keep a roof over our head. I'm positive that my own mother will call me a fool when I tell her that I'm POSITIVE. I'm POSITIVE that when I walk up to the counter and hand over a script with the word Biktarvy on it, that the old dried up pharmacist at the drug store will give me a look that will break me.

This isn't the last time that you're going to here from me, I am going to fight like the bad-ass black woman that I am trying to be. Pick myself up, tighten up these braids and put on a face that keeps the world from pressing down on my shoulders. Problem is, I don't know what I got left to fight with. He played me, he played me hard. Just one last thing, no, not one last thing, I am not ready for one last thing. There will be plenty of things, no last, not yet, this I am POSITIVE of.

The last Swalla' in the Container

Roe Braddy

I don't know why you took it, don't make no sense
what you done to me
Why did you have to go and take the last little bit
that I had. I would have given
You every little drop

You could have left me with somethin' in the
container, just one last swalla'
You took all the best parts, left me with not even a
full taste
Just enough to make ya thirsty and mad

A good soul would leave enough to nourish the spirit,
wet the whistle and breathe
Light into the next dawn, but no_ you left nothin'
Not even a good swalla'

I can't believe that you drank from this vessel, took
from this woman, taking the last swalla'.
You pressed your lips to it, loving it like it was like
your life force
 You whispered
Sweet secrets to it in the middle of the night You
called it your sweet thing

When there was no one lookin' you left it alone for
another one that you claimed was
Full

A little bit of nothin' ain't doing me no good
It don't even reach the back of my throat, that's
the place of my thirst
The place of my hurt that needs to be rubbed hard
and loved soft

But you took it, that last swalla', don't make no
sense, no sense at all

You were bold enough to leave this vessel empty, on
a shelf of pain and loneliness
 when it gave you all it had
It once held your heart, had your babies, rocked
them to sweet slumber into the night
Nursed them with milk that came from the overflow
of its love, you have the nerve to take the
Last swalla'

How dare you take the last swalla' from this
container, this vessel, this woman
You put it back up on the shelf like it didn't mean
nothin' to you. Just as cold as you can be.
You didn't care what this vessel had to offer. You
had the nerve to take the last swalla!

You could have left somethin' to nourish these dry bones, something to lift the spirit
But you went ahead and took the last swalla'

You took from the full container, bleedin' it dry until it had nothing to give,
This cup once overflowed into abundancy, filled to the top
Running over and flowing like spring eternal

Nourishing all that needed it, but then you came along and snatched away its life force
When you took everything, even the last swalla'
The life in it was sweet, the air around it ebbed and flowed to the beat that it sang to
Until the day that you took hold of it
You stole its purpose and passion

You took the last swalla'

Give it back, it don't belong to you no more
It don't make no sense, no sense at all
That was the last swalla'

Loose Wild Young Thang

Roe Braddy

Who do you think you are? Loose wild young thang
Free to dance, free to sing Loving your man child
under my roof, where I labor and rest my head
Dreaming your childish dreams, causing pain to those
who have suffered and scuffled along for your
visions to soar

Who do you think you are? Loose wild young thang,
running wild without a care
Singing songs and pressing your young body to limits
it shouldn't bare
I don't understand this thing that you feel you have
freedom to commit

Here under my roof
Here in the sanctum of my coveted space
Lord Chile, who do you think you are?
Loose young wild thang defiling your body and lying
to yourself

Causing us all this pain. Burning loins, hot on fire
with the passion of a young love that we all once
knew
There's so much more to be had, so much more of
the world to know

Passion knows its place, it's a small amber that scorches holes in your soul

Who do you think you are, loose wild young thang?
I remember young love well, I was young once too
Sweet kisses he ran down my lips and touched my heart with false promises of forever

Chile, open your eyes, listen to these old folks and what they say, they speak truth
Ain't no shame in my game I know what it's like to burn
Go on now, don't forget who you are and whence you came
Blink your eyes hard and wake from this state of insanity that you have placed yourself in
Good sense and closed legs will take you places that you need to find yourself going

I still ask this question; do you know who you are?
Loose wild young thang'

I am a Woman Longing to be...
Roe Braddy

I am a woman longing to be unshackled by the
albatrosses of hatred and pain
Free to find the side of me that boldly walks the
path toward feminism and charity
You see I hale from the tribe of the great migration
A leaderless, but robust revolution

I am a woman longing to be unstoppable, traveling
the path along side the broken, beaten bones of
those who came before me saturated with truth,
speaker of social justice, mindful of the angst of
those who have lost their way

I am a woman longing to take stalk of all that
flourishes near the surface of racial reconciliation,
isolation and bitterness
Riding the world of segregation, desolation and
discontentment
It burns at a fever pitch, this woman I am longing to
be
It scorches a hole in my spirit and at the pit of my
being

I owe it to the young child who sits at my knee to
sow seeds of understanding and discernment

We as a people can not leave it unsaid, words not turned over in futile grown are dead
I will use my voice to make a difference because I am a woman longing to be full of wisdom and truth

I am a woman full of sass, longing to possess finesse, ease and grace
Willing and wanting to give back to mother earth what lies dormant in a waiting womb of contentment
I am a woman longing to be no longer pledged and trapped in a system that continues to only see brown babies and black men as three fourths worth the right to justice and equality

This woman that I am longing to be owns the board room, rules in the court room and finds the savory satisfaction of rest in her home because she is called blessed
This woman that I am longing to be finds comfort in knowing her worth. She speaks of justice
Walks along side of the have nots and the wanna be's

This woman that I am longing to be knows that the color of her skin, the width of her hip, the curl of her hair is not what corporate America sees as politically correct
This woman that I am longing to be loves a man who works with his mind but uses this heart to touch and shape humanity, she is wise in spirit, short on unkind words and long on endurance

This woman that I am longing to be sees all these things and simply longs for them all to just be

Roe Braddy, a playwright, retired teacher, and Pittsburgh native, uses her writing to bring readers into the experiences of her characters. She first brought us into the lives of the children living with disabilities and their teachers in her book, "A Seat on the Playground". In "The Warm Heart of Steele" she draws from her own childhood in the "Steel City", and from the stories she heard many times while growing up in the Hill District. Roe also has a passion for the theatre. "A Warm Heart of Steele" was adapted into a live stage production that was produced and performed in a local community theatre in Harrisburg, PA. She has also written a produced two other stage productions. Roe enjoys writing children's stories that teach life lessons, stories about the Civil Rights era and writing poetry with social justice themes. She is a ferocious reader and loves August Wilson. She likens herself "To becoming the next August Wilson." Roe lives in Pennsylvania with her husband and two adult children

Spring During Corona
Kimmika Williams-Witherspoon

(To the tune of Winter in America by Gil Scott Heron)

And now it's Spring
Spring During corona
And all the people
Infected and dying away.
Lord knows its spring
Spring in America.
And first responders
Done been Killed or betrayed.
And the people know
The people know that
It's spring
Spring during corona
Lord knows its spring in America.
And nobody's fighting
Because nobody knows what to say.

From the empire
Once thought invincible
To the capitalist
With all their gain.
There still be vultures
Circling 'neath the dark clouds
Looking for the rain...

hoping to make more gain...
So many cities
Full of people of color
Just like trees in the forest
No one can hear or see
Never had a chance to grow...
Never had a chance to be.

And now it's Spring
Spring During corona
And all the people
Infected and dying away.
Lord knows its spring
Spring in America.
And first responders
Done been Killed or betrayed.
And the people know
The people know that
It's spring
Spring during corona
Lord knows its spring in America.
And nobody's fighting
Because nobody knows what to say.

And now it's still spring
Spring during corona
The sun now sets on an empire
Shut down in quarantine.
And now it's spring
Spring during corona

And nobody's fighting
Because nobody knows what to think.

While nations struggle
To stop the spread of infection
Hundreds of thousands
Isolated, unable to breathe
Unequal treatment
Weighed 'gainst what's expendable, indeed.
We seethe, and looks like they're hoping
Hoping for some rain.

And I see flowers
Sprouting from my window
While anxious grandmothers
Wave and kiss kids through panes
Social distancing
Slowly turns to ritual
And the departed
Lying in state in freezer trucks
Unscathed by rain.

And now it's Spring
Spring During corona
And all the people
Infected and dying away.

And now it's spring
Spring in America
All of the healers

Done been Killed or betrayed.
And the people know
The people know that
It's spring
Spring during corona
Lord knows its spring in America.
And nobody's fighting
Because nobody knows what to say.
Save your soul
From Spring
Spring during corona
Spring in America
Nobody's fighting
Because no one knows what to say.

Heavy set

Kimmika L. H. Williams-Witherspoon

We see them
Buxomly, Black women who
seemingly
Carry
The weight of the world
On their backs
Or their fronts
Heavy
Body-image
& position in the world
No
Mammy stereotype
Re-envisioned
I saw her today
Her waddled walk
Awkward
Purposeful and
Unforgiven
No modeled penguin
So perfected
Hers
Is not a comical cartoon?
Each step
Rigorous
Laborious and painful
Sidewinding

Cracks and splinters
& boards pulled up
That Langston
Could only write about
Not born
But made bruised
Malformed
By gender
& condition
Black.

Outside My Window

Kimmika L. H. Williams-Witherspoon

Daffodils peek up from the fence 'round the house

Street barren, from the cul de sac down

Station lot 'cross the street

Sparse & quiet

Like dead of winter

'stead, dead of corona—

done in by virus

fearing the known unknown.

Who would have thought

panic over prayer.

Ghost Town: In Quarantine

Kimmika L. H. Williams-Witherspoon

Woke up
Dark
& grey
& grim
another day in
COVID-19
Ex-husband calls
To check in
Always "other-worldly"
Conversation ends with
Confessions
Of a tanker
Container
buried 'tween
Appalachian Mountains
& the Poconos—
Survivalist at its best
on the land of his ex-wife
(Allegedly)
The woman
He cheated on me with
Stuck underground
On her land
In an apocalypse—
The irony be damned!
I couldn't make this shit up

If I tried....

II.

no movement on the street
no greetings when you meet
sometimes in the black, quiet sound
nearly silent footsteps of lone, walking feet
but that's all.
Ghost Town in America—
COVID-19.

III.

During the day
Everything looks normal
Except
There are more cars on the block
For the middle of the week.

At night,
Houselights, from the windows
Echo,
Everyone's doing alright.
Bright lights
& warm glows from T.V.'s through the windows
helps to quell the nightly
fright
focusing on the warmth of the light
as promise
that neighbors are full

& with their families
despite
our world seemingly turned upside down.
COVID-19
Weeks in...
Praying by twilight every night
For God's might
To turn the world
Right-side right
Again.

Kimmika Williams-Witherspoon, Ph.D. Is an Associate Professor of Urban Theater and Community Engagement and Vice President of the Faculty Senate at Temple University, Philadelphia, PA. She is the author of Through Smiles and Tears: The History of African American Theater (From Kemet to the Americas) (Lambert Academic Publishing, 2011); The Secret Messages in African American Theater: Hidden Meaning Embedded in Public Discourse (Edwin Mellen Publishing, 2006). Her stages credits include over 20 productions, 8 one-woman shows and she has performed poetry in over 110 national and international venues. Dr. Williams-Witherspoon is a contributing poet to more than 40 anthologies and author of 11 books of poetry. Her work centers around pedagogy, women's issues, the African diaspora, performance rituals and community engagement.